End Your Self-Sabotage

Library and Archives Canada Cataloguing in Publication

Sangollo, Liane, 1961-
    End Your Self-Sabotage
    1. Motivation (Psychology). 2. Success – Psychological aspect.

Issued in print and electronic formats

ISBN: 978-0-9949508-4-0 (paperback) ISBN: 978-0-9949508-5-7 (eBook)

MY COACH AND I PRESS

Originally published as *Démystifier votre imposteur :
Les 8 saboteurs qui vous empêchent d'avoir la vie que
vous voulez*

Cover design: Emilie Robert

Back cover photo: Emilie Robert

Cover illustration: Depositphotos

Printed in the USA

Liane Sangollo
CHRP, PCC

End Your Self-Sabotage

8 Deadly Patterns
Preventing You from
Leading the Life You
Want

This book is dedicated to my father, who taught me the importance of following my heart and trusting my instincts.

Table of Contents

Acknowledgments

I would like to thank, first and foremost, all the people who have worked with me and placed their trust in me over the past twenty years. They have shared intimate details about themselves, their situations and their experiences. They chose to make changes in their lives, and mapped an individual path for doing so.

I would also like to thank my family, as well as my friends and colleagues, past and present, for their love and support.

Writing this book has prompted me to constantly question myself, to progress, to evolve and, most importantly, to take responsibility for the way in which I want to live my life.

Finally, I am very grateful to Lisette, who was my life coach, my spiritual guide and my friend. She had a significant influence on me: she enabled me to believe in myself and to see that we all have the power to change.

Notice to the Reader

This is the first book I've written. I tackled it with a great deal of motivation and passion.

It is intended for people who are questioning their life choices and habits, who want to go beyond the status quo, make changes and move forward, who want to believe in happiness.

But what is happiness? What are the self-defeating patterns that prevent us from achieving the life we want to live?

Foreword

We all have a number of self-defeating patterns, which can be subtle yet ever present. In this book, I describe some of these patterns and illustrate them through real-life cases.* I then suggest a series of exercises that can be used to help overcome them.

If we want to work on ourselves and make changes, we need to think about the life we want to live, and become aware of how we're standing in our own way. To identify and overcome our self-defeating patterns, it's essential for us to discover what they bring out in us.

When I coach people, I rely on the usual methodology, which is to pinpoint the person's goal, ask impactful questions to help him or her become conscious of the obstacles, give feedback to clarify points, encourage the person and reinforce change, and provide exercises to ensure the action plan is successful.

That same methodology is reflected in this book, which I hope will help readers understand the origin of self-defeating patterns and come to recognize and overcome some of the different aspects of self-sabotage.

---

* The names and professions of the people discussed have been changed in order to protect their privacy.

Introduction

We think that happiness is impossible in some situations. But even in difficult times, we need to hold onto our zest for life and our determination to effect change.

We have to keep faith that we can shape the future. Every life experience enables us to learn something constructive. The ability to be happy is within all of us.

It's no coincidence that I entitled this book *End Your Self-Sabotage*. I have been a victim of my own self-defeating patterns many times in my life, not taking responsibility for my happiness. I have blamed others for my actions and my life decisions. Believe me, I still have to work hard every day to build the life I want.

We all have the potential to realize that we are responsible for the choices we make and that we can have what we want in life to make ourselves happy, regardless of our situation. How do we stand in our own way? What is behind our self-defeating patterns?

As a former human resources manager and present professional coach, I've had the opportunity to work with a number of people. I wanted to share some of their real-life experiences.

I decided to focus specifically on what prevents us from overcoming our self-defeating patterns and pursuing our goals. What prevents us from being our true selves? Why can't we see what we have to do to take responsibility for the life we want to live?

The good news is that we can stand back, take a look at ourselves, and think about our life choices.

What do we expect from life? What do we want from each and every area of our lives? From our relationships, our jobs, our families, our personal activities? What do we want in terms of our health and financial well-being? What does this mean on a day-to-day basis?

If we want to change, we must find the answers to these and other questions. That requires a positive attitude, an open mind, and the ability to take action.

It's all in the wanting.

We all have our particular values, training, experience and concept of happiness.

However, we have to bear in mind that we are our own masters, we are the architects of our lives. We have the tools to make the changes we desire. We have what we need to realize our full potential, because we are creative.

So, what is our responsibility toward ourselves and others? What do we do with it?

Are you ready? To take responsibility for your fate and demystify your self-defeating patterns?

1

Understanding Self-Sabotage

Self-sabotage stems primarily from a lack of self-esteem. Self-esteem is made up of:

- self-worth or self-love;
- self-acceptance;
- self-confidence; and
- self-perception.

I discuss self-esteem and define its components in chapter two. But first, I'd like to outline the self-defeating behavioural patterns we unconsciously engage in every day.

Through my work as a human resources manager and professional coach, I have detected eight deadly patterns, which are as follows:

- wanting to be right;
- feeling guilty;
- being judgmental and blaming others;
- playing the victim;
- being afraid;
- making excuses;
- having expectations;
- not living in the present.

Wanting to be right

"If you never assume importance, you never lose it."

Tao Te Ching

I love this quote. What, in fact, is behind wanting to be right?

Understanding what being right is about

In any situation, you can ask yourself: Am I right? Does that make sense?

For people who are self-satisfied, being right may be a way of indicating to their peers that they are recognized, credible and respected. In my opinion, it's a way of aggrandizing oneself, of saying, "I'm smarter than everyone" or "I'm the best." It's as if the person is convinced that he or she holds the truth about a particular situation or issue. In fact,

Wanting to be right can be a form of resistance.

It can generate conflict and may reflect insecurity.

Why would someone want to be right at all costs? Why would someone have an overblown view of himself or herself? Wanting to be right is a form of vanity. What is "vanity"? It's conceit, but it also refers to something that is futile or unreal. We see the world through the tiny prism of the self. While that may be real to us, it would be vain to overlook all other points of view. That's what we tend to do every day.

Real-life case

Tom, a representative of a large international brokerage firm

Tom is considered to be one of the best representatives in his firm. For the past five years, he has garnered the award for performance excellence.

He came to see me because he wanted to work on his interpersonal relations. Despite his strong performance record, his immediate superior had criticized him for not being sufficiently open and attentive to his colleagues.

During our first meeting, Tom was quick to tell me about his professional achievements.

At another session, he told me about a situation he'd experienced. He explained that, for the past seven years, he and his colleagues had attended a conference on business development.

At the last conference, he met a man named Jim, who was sitting at his table. Jim was fifty-seven and an entrepreneur. They started talking about their jobs, and specifically discussed the impact of the economic crisis on business development.

During their conversation, Tom voiced his opinions on the issue. Jim also expressed his views, which were different from Tom's.

Tom told me that his take on the issue was right. "I'm bright. I'm well known in my field even though I'm young. I've won awards. My performance is solid as a rock. I thought Jim was wrong."

Tom heard what Jim was saying, but wasn't really listening to him. Tom underestimated Jim.

Then he told me that he deliberately, although discreetly, started talking to the others at the table because he didn't want to continue the conversation with Jim. After the meal, he left to attend the afternoon sessions.

I asked Tom—as I do all the people who consult me—questions designed to help him become aware of his motivations and behaviours that have an impact on his goal. Here are some of those questions:

🗨 *Impactful questions*

- What is your motivation for being right?
- What were you resisting in the situation with Jim?
- What's behind this perception?
- How do you feel when people express views that differ from your own?
- What makes you think that you're not credible?
- How does your wanting to be right affect the people around you (friends, family, colleagues)?
- What makes you think that your colleagues don't have a good opinion of you?
- How are you going to start welcoming the comments and views of others at meetings without criticizing them?

Tom's attitude—believing that he was right—affected his interpersonal relations not only at work, but in all areas of his life.

⦿ *Realizations*

- Tom's answers to these questions helped him identify his blocks. Through our discussions, Tom came to realize that he was putting up resistance both to himself and to others. He was focused on his perception of things, his inflated ego and his beliefs. He downplayed the views of others and the importance of their experience.

His inability to see himself and his situation contributed to his short-sightedness about others. He realized that other people also have relevant beliefs, perceptions and views of situations and events. This prompted him to start thinking differently.

> ≪ By taking a step back, we can get a different perspective on a situation.

- Tom realized that wanting to be right was a way of masking insecurity. He was afraid that others might ridicule him, especially since he was young. He desperately wanted to assert his views, thinking that it would make him appear more credible. He had worked hard to get where he was. He imposed his views not only to take a stand, but to prove that he existed.

After giving the matter much thought and coming to certain realizations, Tom humbly admitted that Jim had raised some good points about how to get out of the economic crisis and that his views made sense.

During our meetings, I asked Tom simply to welcome the opinions of his colleagues, actively listen to them, and discuss matters with them.

I actually asked him to listen to what other people have to say and to let himself to be swayed by their arguments. I also asked him to be attentive to the emotions he experienced and to see if he felt insecure about how others perceive him.

> « Going beyond the confines of our beliefs isn't threatening.

Tom became aware of his motivation for wanting to be right; he now has the tools to deal with the situation. He was able to stand back, take a look at himself, and admit that Jim had made some relevant comments. He acknowledged that there was nothing to be insecure about. He has to work on his self-perception, which is part of self-esteem.

Can you identify with Tom? Can you see yourself in his situation?

We all have our own perceptions, opinions, aspirations, beliefs and ways of reacting to issues and to our environment, be it personal or professional. We interpret everything through this prism.

So why would we insist on being right? Think about it!

I'm not saying that we should stop voicing our opinions. I'm simply saying that we can assert ourselves without sidelining others; we can keep an open mind. Is it so difficult to be open to the views of others?

When I read the paper or watch the news, I wonder how many leaders and politicians want to be right despite disagreement and differences, to make strategic choices and to maintain their decisions, even if they have a negative impact on citizens, the economy and the country.

I wonder if those present at their discussion table really supported their decisions. What would have happened had they voiced opposition? Would they have lost their positions despite their value?

Are decisions made for the benefit of leaders and politicians themselves or for the benefit of society? At what cost?

Some people believe that they are above criticism in their handling of power. They overrate themselves in the way they exercise leadership, possibly to meet their own needs. And yet, some of them are paying the price today. But we're also paying the price for having placed our trust in them!

My father used to say, "Give a person power and I'll tell you what he's made of!"

We all have a share of responsibility in the actions taken, be they on an environmental, social or other level.

👤 *Real-life case*

Mark, a programmer

Mark stood out from the time he was very young because he was so bright. He learned quickly and was ahead of the others in school. His teachers had to find ways to keep him stimulated and engaged. He started reading books before he'd even learned to read. His parents told him he was good, intelligent and that he would go far in life. His self-esteem and self-worth were based on his intellect. He had few friends.

Mark came to see me because he wanted help in developing relationships, particularly with women. He didn't really know how to go about it. For a number of years, he'd been focusing all his attention on setting up new games for a specialized firm. He had difficulty approaching the opposite sex and hadn't had much success with women since he was a teen. He'd had relationships, but they were very short-lived and noncommittal.

At our first session, he said to me, "I have trouble meeting women even though I have a high IQ. Maybe that's the problem. I have colleagues who are not as bright, yet they're popular with the ladies."

Before we continue, let's look at the abilities measured by IQ tests. IQ tests assess cognitive skills: language, mathematics, spatial perception and reasoning. They don't include sensitivity, emotions or interpersonal skills, which are assessed by EQ (emotional intelligence quotient) tests.

Possessing emotional intelligence doesn't make someone better than others. However, it can enable them to use their personal and social skills optimally in their relations with others.

☰ *Impactful questions*

- How can you suggest that your self-worth is related solely to your IQ?
- What makes you believe that, because of your IQ, you can't start up conversations with others?
- How do you feel when you first meet someone?
- How do you introduce yourself?
- What topics do you discuss when you first meet people?
- On a scale of 1 to 10, how would you rate your ability to listen to others?
- What do your colleagues have over you that enables them to communicate effectively with others?
- What would you like to experience with someone? Name five main things.

Realizations

- Mark realized that he thought others should be as intelligent as he is. He believed he was better than others, both men and women. The reason he couldn't develop relationships or maintain friendships was because he underestimated people.
- It's important to note that he felt anxious and uncomfortable about meeting people. He felt awkward and didn't really know what to say. So he would introduce himself as a games expert and talk about himself, because he didn't feel threatened when he did so. He realized that he only asked questions about gaming and wasn't concerned about asking people about their interests.

Mark started to see new potential for improving his well-being. He needed to re-evaluate some of his beliefs. He realized that his colleagues had interpersonal skills and abilities. They worked easily as a team, were open to others, had social interaction, showed empathy, listened actively and cooperated with others.

I asked Mark to work on his emotional self. Did he have good self-awareness? Was he able to feel his own emotions?

First, he had to detect and recognize his emotions. That was difficult: he had to learn how to open up to himself and accept himself. Then, he had to get to know himself and discover his worth, which was not based only on his intellect.

As he gets to know himself better, he'll be able to change what's preventing him from achieving what he really wants. He'll also be better able to manage his emotions.

If we want to achieve a high level of self-awareness, it's vital for us to face what we feel. Our greatest obstacle to increased self-awareness is avoiding what we feel, rather than facing it head-on.

🔹 *Real-life case*

Luke, a businessman

Luke had owned several clothing boutiques over a fifteen-year period and had supervised a large portion of the sales force. For various reasons, including management issues and economic downturns, he'd had to close them. After giving the matter much thought, he had decided to go to work for someone else.

He came to see me for assistance in preparing for an upcoming interview. As we talked, I learned that he'd worked for several employers in the previous two years. Clearly he was having trouble holding down a job. I dug deeper, trying to find out why.

🔹 *Impactful questions*

- Why haven't you been able to hold onto your last few jobs?
- What's the challenge that you're facing right now?
- How do you feel about having a boss now instead of being the one in charge?
- What emotions do you experience when your ideas are not accepted?
- If you talked and listened to others, how would that affect your work?
- What would you gain by having a different attitude?
- What would you be risking if you don't change your attitude?
- What can you do to correct this situation?

Realizations

- Luke had not kept his last few jobs because they weren't what he wanted. He had become impatient in certain situations and reacted too quickly. He thought his colleagues all behaved in essentially the same way: they didn't collaborate with him. "You know," he told me, "I'm an expert in sales. I won't have them telling me how to do it."

- He stood up to everyone he worked with. He had difficulty taking orders from his immediate superior.

- Luke let his emotions and perceptions influence his behaviour. He was in conflict with his colleagues.

- He admitted that the transition from boss to employee was a difficult one.

- He also admitted that when his own employees had made suggestions or comments about sales or other matters, he'd heard them but not really listened. He'd been impatient on many occasions, and had had trouble containing himself. In short, he'd always had the last word.

- Luke now feels disempowered and ridiculed by others. He had spent a good part of his professional life managing his own business and doing what he wanted. He realized that he hadn't grieved that loss. And yet, he was the one who made the decision to work for someone else. That meant that he had to adjust and follow the rules of the company he worked for.

- He had to stop thinking that he was right, and learn how to be patient and listen with empathy. He also had to avoid seeking confrontation. If he didn't change his attitude, he wouldn't be able to hold onto a job.

He had to accept himself the way he is and be open to others.

Helping people improve their self-awareness involves helping them to better understand certain perceptions (such as biases) and grasp what they're unable to see.

Luke's goal in coming to see me changed during our first meeting. That's something that often happens. It's important for me to ask the right questions in order to see what's behind the person's goal.

Should we stop always wanting to be right? I don't think so; nor should we accept always being wrong either. It's a question of being able to remain open in our relations with others. That is a vital quality.

Exercise

OPENING UP TO OTHERS

1. Take a few deep breaths before each of your meetings.

2. When involved in discussions with others, listen to what they say and take an interest in them.

3. Don't focus on yourself. Ask open-ended questions like "Why do you think that?" or "How do you see the situation?" Benefit from other people's views.

4. Give people feedback on their opinions and comments by saying things like "Yes, that's an option" or "Can you show me what you mean?"

5. Pause for a moment and try to discern how that makes you feel. Name the emotion and determine how you are reacting to it.

6. Simply give your objective opinion without thinking, *There's no way we're doing that. I'm the one who's right here.* Remain neutral.

7. Listen attentively to other people's arguments without judging them. Other viewpoints enable you to see different aspects of a situation. Be open and understanding when it comes to human behaviour.

8. Afterwards, try to take a critical look at yourself and at how you could have done things differently. Try to be as objective as possible.

REMEMBER: When we strive to impose our truth on others and to prove to ourselves and others that we exist, we're showing a lack of self-perception (see chapter two for the relationship between self-perception and self-esteem).

> Gaining objectivity is one of the greatest challenges in gaining self-awareness.

Objectivity enables you to see all facets of yourself.

Keep a journal, and write down your feelings as they arise.

It's also important to be aware of your physical reactions to situations. Do you have sweaty hands? Do you tap your feet or sigh? How do you control these reactions?

If you do this exercise for several months, it'll give you a clearer view of yourself and others.

Yes, it requires discipline, patience and courage. But the results will be worth it.

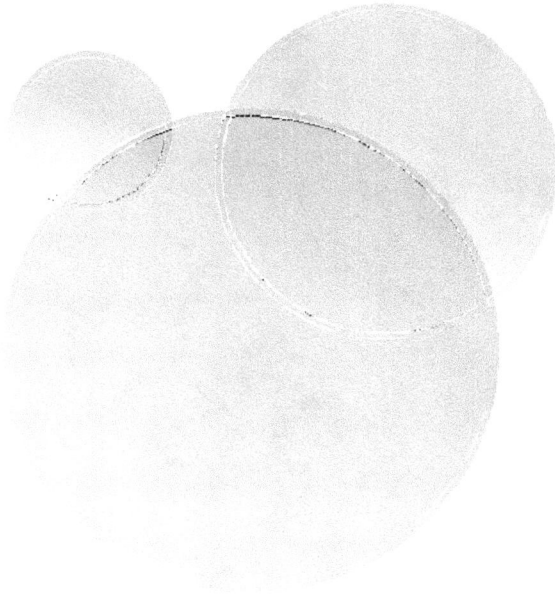

Feeling guilty

"Taking responsibility is listening to your own conscience; feeling guilty is listening to someone else's."

Ghislain Devroede

How many times have you said or heard things like "That's my fault!" "I shouldn't have said that!" "I shouldn't have done that!" "I don't have any excuse!" "My colleague seems ticked off; she's not calling me back." "Is it something I said?"

In your meeting with your colleague, did you clearly establish your position on the matter discussed? Were you consistent in your responses? Or did you feel inferior? What is feeling inferior about?

How many times have we heard our parents say, "You can't wear that!" "You look terrible!" "You're being ridiculous!" What are the repercussions of such disparaging remarks repeated over the years? Do we develop a poor self-image? As adults, we punish ourselves with the same derogatory messages: "I look terrible!" I'm being ridiculous!"

The facets of guilt
We've all done something we regret and then had to come to terms with ourselves or someone else.

At one point, I intentionally hurt my spouse because he'd said something inappropriate that hurt me. Then I felt guilty. What I did to my spouse was deliberate and against my principles. I was able to take back what I said and apologize.

Can we feel guilty day in and day out? It would take enormous energy to think about everything we say or do that might hurt someone. Feeling guilty is a reflection of how we see ourselves in relation to others. We may be selling ourselves short if we constantly feel that we're letting others down.

Imagine how many times we refrain from taking action that would enable us to meet our own needs.

There are many people who anticipate feeling guilty. As a result, they avoid saying or doing something for fear of bothering people.

Can you recall an incident in which you saw a sibling or friend get hurt and cry? Then later, when talking with your loved one about what had happened, did you feel empathy? Did you feel guilty for not doing something in that situation?

Sometimes, an exaggerated need to help others can result from feelings of guilt.

I remember seeing my parents quarrel, and it made me sad. I thought they were going to separate and that I was to blame. I felt guilty because I wasn't able to do anything about it. My guilty feelings were based on a misperception.

« Not able to do something = Feeling guilty

When we become adults, do we feel guilty because we're unable to assert ourselves appropriately, to defend ourselves?

Do we ever feel that we're not able to accomplish a given task, then acknowledge feeling guilty for not going through with it?

Conversely, if we feel guilty, that can prevent us from being able to take action or move forward.

Here's an example of "not doing something and feeling guilty." A few years ago, my ex-spouse and I wanted to undertake a project together. We had an opportunity to buy land. We discussed how we would manage the project and the impact it would have on our lifestyle.

The project prompted us to discuss our values, what was important to us. We talked about it for several months. My spouse proposed different options, but I was ambivalent.

In the end, I decided not to do the project with him because of finances and the fact that I was just starting other new initiatives. He was relying on my financial participation in the venture.

Because I opted out, he missed an opportunity that arose and had to delay certain purchases. He also had to find another partner.

When I told him I wasn't going in with him, he was frustrated. He clearly expressed his feelings by sighing and being curt with me. He said to me directly, "I understand why you've decided against it, but you could've told me a long time ago."

I felt bad about it. I started to justify my decision as if I were on trial. To tell the truth, I felt guilty for having said no to him.

When I justified why I had decided not to join him in the venture, I had a physical reaction. My heart was pounding, my hands were sweating, I spoke quickly and my voice was high-pitched. I was emotional, and paced back and forth.

Then I went for a walk in the woods by the house, slowly calmed down, and eventually felt like myself again.

The questions I asked myself were as follows:

- What was my motivation for justifying myself?
- Why did I feel guilty?
- Why did I have difficulty accepting the situation?
- Did I feel that I'd made the right decision for me?
- Why was I reacting so strongly?

I realized that the love that came with my spouse's approval was important to me. I wanted to be sure that he wouldn't leave me. Had I disappointed someone I loved? I realized that I'd been raised to please others and that I'd continued that behaviour as an adult.

What was important in this situation was for me to act according to what I believed. The only person who was disappointed was *me*. Did I really have to justify myself? No. I simply had to be clear within myself. I had to provide an explanation for my decision, defend my point of view—that's all! I had to respect myself. As mentioned, self-respect is part of self-love.

When we act in keeping with ourselves and feel that we've made the right decision, it's up to us to hold onto that feeling and not sink into a quagmire of guilt.

Real-life case

Denise, a sales rep

When Denise contacted me, she said she wanted to learn how to be more assertive. That, she said, would have an impact on certain choices she would make concerning her family.

We met at a restaurant at her convenience. During the meal, I noticed that every time Denise asked the waiter for something, she prefaced her request. For example, she would say, "I'm sorry to bother you, but could you please bring me another glass of wine?" or "I know I'm being a pain, but could you please bring me some more bread?" I was surprised by what she said when she ordered.

I thought about the words she used. She sounded as if she felt guilty, but that seemed odd. She didn't want to bother the waiter, but that was his job!

How many times have we not sent a restaurant meal back to the kitchen simply because we didn't want to bother the staff or displease them? How many times have we not returned a bottle of wine even though it was off? We pay for these products and services. How many times has a waiter asked us if the meal is to our liking and we've answered, "Yes, it's very good," without admitting what's wrong with it? We think to ourselves that there's no point in saying anything because we won't be going back. What do we feel guilty about? How do we think we look to these people? Is our image at stake? We have a responsibility to assert ourselves.

Coming back to Denise, I said, "So, you're a pain." She nodded and looked at me inquisitively. She was in the habit of saying that when she ordered something at a restaurant, but was unaware that she felt guilty. I asked her some questions about it.

📰 *Impactful questions*

- Why do you say, "I know I'm a pain, but could you..."?
- What are you feeling when you say that?
- How do you see yourself?
- How would you like to feel when you go to a restaurant?
- What's the waiter's role?

I suggested that she call the waiter over and ask him for something else, without saying, "I'm sorry to bother you or I know I'm a pain."

🧠 *Realizations*

- Denise was unaware of the impact of such statements. She felt guilty for bothering the waiter and didn't want to displease him.

- It reminded her of situations in her family where she had felt sorry and rejected after asking for things she thought were troublesome to her parents.

- Denise realized that it was not her fault if the waiter felt bothered or ill-humoured because of her requests for food or drink.

- She simply wanted to relax, enjoy a delicious meal, and not stress if she ordered more. She realized that she approached her family in the same way. She had to take a look at her self-perception and her sense of self-worth.

The key is awareness. When we assert ourselves, we realize that the guilty feelings disappear.

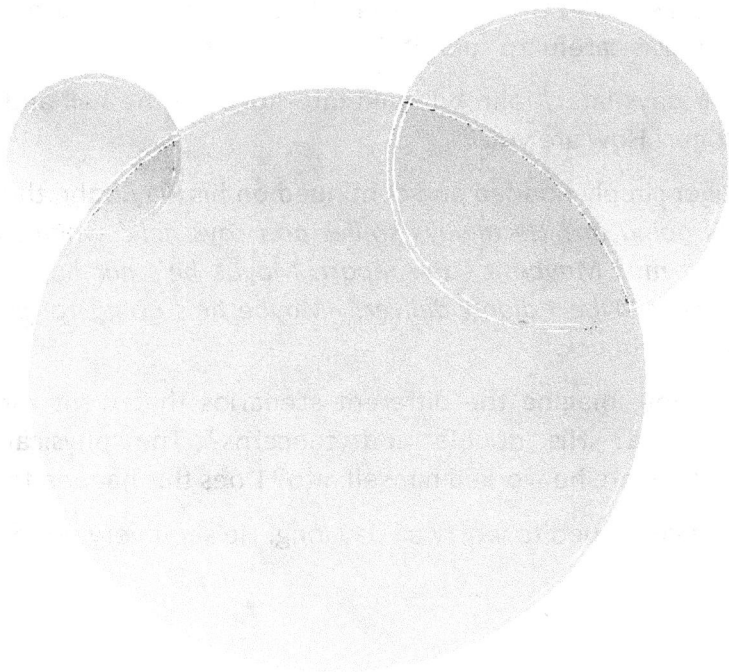

Real-life case

John, an accounting technician

During our first meeting, John told me that his goal was to be more open to other people's reactions without feeling targeted or attacked.

John had been working in the accounting department of a consulting firm for two years. His immediate superior, Roger, the Director of Finance, asked him to prepare an urgent report. John worked on the report day and night for a week.

He was proud of his research, data analysis and turnaround plan. He was careful to submit the report on time.

Two days later, John bumped into Roger in the hall and said, "Hi, Roger! How are you?"

Roger simply nodded and continued on his way. John thought, *What's going on? He always smiles and says hello when I greet him. Is it me? Maybe it's the report. Maybe he's not happy with the work. Maybe I didn't deliver... Maybe he's going to give me negative feedback.*

Can you imagine the different scenarios that went through John's mind? His doubts and concerns? The physical and emotional state he worked himself into? Does this happen to you?

John continued to worry all day long. He slept very poorly that night.

The next day, he was anxious when he got to the office. He wondered what would happen when he saw Roger.

To his surprise, Roger wasn't there. He'd left the office the previous afternoon because his brother had sustained an accident and been rushed to hospital.

How many times have we imagined scenarios? How many times have we reacted to situations we've merely envisioned? Do you know how much energy that consumes?

In this case, John worried for nothing. He was unable to interpret Roger's reaction, so he somehow assumed that he had done something wrong, that it was his fault.

John had to work on his self-confidence.

☰ *Impactful questions*

- How would you rate your self-confidence on a scale of 1 to 10?
- Why did you give yourself 6.5? What do you think of yourself?
- What type of thoughts have you been thinking since the situation with Roger?
- Can you write a list of your personal and professional achievements in the past five years?
- What have you learned about yourself in the past five years?
- Can you name and note five skills, strengths or abilities that you possess?
- How did you feel when you told me about your achievements?
- How are you perceived by your colleagues?
- What do you need to change about yourself to gain confidence?
- What other options might you consider?

🔮 *Realizations*

I asked John to read me the list of his achievements, strengths and abilities.

- John became aware of all his potential. His list of accomplishments and qualities was very impressive. He saw himself as competent and wanted to do a little more. He also realized that his colleagues like him.

- He acknowledged that he's generous, enjoys working with others as a team, and is a good leader. After reading the list, he felt serene. He now had to stop doubting himself and start believing in himself.

- When he was a child, people would say things to him like "I want you to do that over. That's not good enough. You have to start applying yourself."

- Those things had an impact on him: he felt he didn't measure up. He became more aware of how he'd been reacting, including to the incident at the office.

- John needed to focus on his strengths. He became aware of the habits he'd developed in childhood when his parents had put him down.

Did he have any reason to feel guilty about the report he submitted to Roger? Absolutely not!

He had to become more confident in his ability to take action. That confidence comes with positive self-esteem.

Many people have difficulty expressing who they are and realizing what they've accomplished. We get drawn into a dynamic without understanding the reactions we've integrated.

🦶 *Real-life case*

Sylvie, a single mother
of three young adults

Sylvie wanted to learn how to set certain boundaries so she could feel good in her relationship with her daughters.

She told me that every time her daughters needed money, they called her because their father would never give it to them.

Sylvie would initially be irritated and object, but would then give in.

She knew that her daughters should be able to manage on their own. However, she was unable to refuse them because she was a single mother and felt guilty about it.

Her daughters had gone through rough times at home when she and her husband experienced marital troubles and a difficult separation.

Since her daughters had lived with her only one week out of two, Sylvie had tried to compensate by giving them everything.

She didn't encourage them to take responsibility for themselves. As a result, she also disempowered herself.

Although Sylvie's daughters were adults and had jobs, they still asked their mother for financial assistance.

Sylvie continued to give in to their requests for money.

☰ *Impactful questions*

- Why do you feel guilty?
- Why are you responsible for giving your daughters money every time they ask?
- What is your daughters' motivation for requesting money?
- How do you feel when your daughters ask you for money?
- Why do you allow this situation to continue?
- What would you like the situation to be like three months from now?
- What measures do you need to take to make that happen?
- What difficulties do you fear would arise if you stopped giving your daughters money?
- How are you going to stop this vicious circle?

⚛ *Realizations*

- Sylvie realized that she was easing her guilty conscience by giving her daughters financial support. However, she also realized that they didn't love her just because she gave them everything they asked for. She felt frustrated and burdened by having to give them money whenever they asked for it.
- She feared that her daughters would react negatively if she said no to them and that they might be upset with her. She didn't like that feeling.
- Sylvie made a decision: to talk to her daughters about the relationship she wanted to have with them.
- She offered to help them draw up a budget (remember, her daughters all have jobs).

She took one step at a time. Sylvie found it difficult at some points, because her daughters came back and asked her for financial assistance several times.

Sylvie declined and did not budge from her position, even though her daughters were unhappy about it.

It took Sylvie some time to put her foot down and not feel guilty about it. She was ultimately able to assert herself and get beyond the situation.

She had to learn how to listen to her own needs and to respect herself. This is another aspect of self-esteem.

« It's important to bear in mind
that everyone makes
changes at their own pace.

Exercise

TO BECOME AWARE OF
YOUR GUILTY FEELINGS

1. At the end of every day, think of the times you felt guilty that day.

2. Regardless of what you said or did or the reasons why, ask yourself, "Do I agree with what I said or did? Why?"

3. Write down the answer, because that will enable you to see what triggered your guilty feelings. Be sure to indicate the time of day the situation occurred.

4. How did you feel when it happened? Can you pinpoint the emotion?

5. How did you react during the situation?

6. Why did you react that way?

7. Take the time to review your responsibility in the situation and that of the other person.

8. Start by writing, "I chose to..."

9. If you had it to do over, what would you do differently?

Take time to listen to the messages you give yourself when you feel guilty (and might be fearing rejection, for example), because it's important to be aware of them.

Be faithful to yourself and the choices you want to make. You'll be surprised by how others respond.

Accept the fact that you're not responsible for others. You're responsible only for your own thoughts, words and deeds.

REMEMBER: We need to become aware of false guilt. When we let go of those feelings, we gain the freedom to be ourselves.

> The important thing is to respect yourself.
> Self-respect = self-love.

Being judgmental and blaming others

"If you're not part of the problem, you're not part of the solution."

It's easy to judge other people. In so doing, we make a judgment about ourselves. We might criticize someone for something they've done, for their attitude or a weakness. We might blame them for a situation or an incident.

What is it that bothers us? Why do we have a problem with differences?

We're different from other people. We don't have the same social status, personality, strengths, weaknesses, and so on.

Could we possibly do the same thing as someone we're judging? Say, for example, one of our colleagues handed in his or her report a couple of days late last month. Could that happen to us this month?

How many times have we thought, *She spends far too much on her appearance. He works way too hard. She's constantly cleaning the house.* At the same time, we avoid acknowledging the things that we're excessive about, be it training, smoking or drinking. If I judge a person for overeating, for example, maybe that's my way of saying that I don't eat very much.

If a person thinks or acts differently from us, which is normal because we're all different, we might say that *our* way of thinking or doing things is better. That's when we're being judgmental. Ironically, maybe we used to think or act the same way as the very person we're now judging.

Conversely, if someone thinks or acts the same way as we do, maybe we find that all well and good. Maybe we find that reassuring.

When we were children and our parents caught us doing something wrong, we'd immediately point a finger at a sibling or friend and say, "It's his fault. He's the one who started it!"

Take time to listen to yourself and those around you. If someone says, for example, "Did you see the *simpleton* who closed the highway with orange cones during rush hour?" he or she is judging the situation without having all the facts.

If someone says, "It's my parents' fault that I'm like this," they may be judging or blaming their folks, but they're certainly not taking responsibility for themselves.

Haven't we said or heard someone at work say, "He's incompetent," "He's incapable of..." "Did you see what he's wearing?" "He thinks he's better than everyone else."

Seeing someone act differently from ourselves is troubling. Admitting that we're troubled by difference is something else altogether: it's like admitting that we think we're better.

How many times do we judge people in a day? When I give presentations on leadership, I like to show participating managers my illustration of Lucky Luke, the cartoon character who shoots faster than his shadow. They find it funny, because it makes them realize how quick to judge or blame they can be.

***

One day, I witnessed an accident in the parking lot of a grocery store. I was sitting in my car waiting for my spouse, who was in the store shopping. I saw a man drive into a parking spot not far from mine. To correct his angle, he had to back up, then drive into the spot again. While he was backing up, a man in the parking spot directly behind his backed out of his spot very quickly. Neither was watching where he was going and they hit each other.

I can still hear them accusing each other in angry tones. "Why didn't you look where you were going? Are you crazy or what? Who do you think you are? This is your fault! Look at what you've done to my car!"

- Why was it the other man's fault?
- What was the first man's motive for saying so?
- What emotions did this incident spark?
- What could the two of them have done to prevent the situation?

Had they both adopted a responsible attitude and calmly admitted that they hadn't looked where they were going, would conversation and tone have been different?

🔰 *Real-life case*

A couple of professionals

A few years ago, I was invited to a friend's house for dinner. There I met a couple who started joking about a trip they had recently taken.

The husband had wanted to go on a cruise and had proposed the idea to his wife. They discussed it, and she admitted that she didn't want to go on a boat. She later agreed to the trip, thinking that it would be exciting to take a different type of vacation.

Enthusiastic about their holiday, the couple reserved a seven-day Caribbean cruise in November.

When they got to the airport, they learned that their flight had been delayed for two hours because of a mechanical problem.

The wife looked at the husband and said, "We haven't even left and already there's a problem!"

The husband tried to lighten the mood and be positive, saying that they'd still get to where they were going.

They did, in fact, get to the boat in time. When they entered their cabin, they were surprised to see that they didn't have the balcony they'd reserved. The wife was very unhappy about that. They were given another cabin with a balcony, but then they ran into bad weather, and the wife got seasick.

The wife made one negative comment after another about the trip, and blamed it all on her husband because he was the one who had proposed the idea in the first place.

☰ *Impactful questions (for the wife)*

- Why did you take the cruise?
- How did you feel about the problems that arose on the ship?
- To what extent were those problems your husband's fault since, as you know, you made the decision with him to take the trip?

How often does something like this happen in our personal or professional lives? What's the impact? It creates conflict and dissatisfaction, and means that we're not taking responsibility for the decisions we make.

When I thought about this couple, I felt compelled to take a look at myself. I admit that I've blamed my spouse in certain situations. Still today, I have to make a point of thinking long and hard before I make a decision.

《《 Understanding the other person
makes us more tolerant.

🔲 *Real-life case*

Top Model Show

I recently saw the show *Top Model*. There were five finalists and the winner would receive a trip to London.

One of the finalists doubted that she could go any further in the competition and was thinking of dropping out because she didn't feel up to the challenge. This was obviously good news for the other contestants because she was a threat. She had a nice personality, was extremely beautiful and very natural.

When she met with the judges, they stressed the fact that her photos were fantastic and that she had enormous potential. They asked her why she underestimated herself and why she was reluctant to continue.

She said she was afraid that she wasn't up to the challenge. The judges pointed out that they were there to guide all the finalists, encourage them and support them through the competition. After all, the contestants were only eighteen years old!

When she returned to the house, the other four finalists asked her how her meeting with the judges went. She replied enthusiastically, "Really well! They think my photos are great and that I have a lot of potential. I don't think I'm going to drop out after all." The judges had given her the encouragement she needed.

One of the finalists started to cry, and the girl asked her why she was crying. Another finalist replied, "It's your fault. You told us you were dropping out of the competition. It's your fault that she's crying. You raised her expectations! You told us you were leaving and now you're going to stay!"

☰ *Impactful questions*

- Why were the girls having trouble giving the competition their best?
- Why did the girls blame the beautiful finalist who had considered dropping out?
- Why were the girls so envious of her?
- What were the consequences for blaming her?

The beautiful finalist was a rival for the others. She had talent and a good chance of winning the competition. The girls were responsible for doing the work and achieving results. It was easy for them to blame her. In fact, she could have blamed them for not taking responsibility and making the necessary effort to win the competition.

The girl who blamed the beautiful finalist was ultimately disqualified because she didn't meet the judges' requirements. In the end, the one who doubted herself but listened to the judges won the competition and the trip to London.

🪪 *Real-life case*

Anthony, a woodworker

Anthony was just entering semi-retirement. He came to see me because he wanted to start managing the time he devoted to his various activities differently. During our conversations, Anthony told me what he thought of his friends, and revealed certain prejudices about inactive people.

"I don't want to die by inches. I find that people my age sit around and do nothing. They should keep doing some sort of work and get some exercise. My friends can't keep up with me at this point. It's really too bad, because they'd benefit from being more active. They're crazy: they spend their entire days in front of their computers or TVs. They're lazy. They don't do anything. Life's so short. Why waste it?"

📰 *Impactful questions*

- What do you feel when you talk about your friends?
- What bothers you about how they choose to live their lives?
- What makes you say that they're lazy?
- How would you like to manage your time?
- Which activities are the most important to you?
- How much time would you like to devote to them?
- What steps are you going to take to ensure you spend the planned time on these activities?

Even if Anthony's goal was to manage his time differently, I wanted to demystify some of the judgments he made during our conversations.

⚛ *Realizations*

- Anthony was afraid of getting old. He wanted to remain vital, maintain his energy, and keep his zest for life, especially now that he was entering semi-retirement.

- Anthony reorganized his activities, determining what was important to him now and what wasn't. He didn't want to feel like an old man with limitations.

- He realized that he'd said his friends were lazy because he felt frustrated: he wanted to age well and have as much time as possible to do things with them. He was worried that he wouldn't meet people through the new activities he'd chosen.

- He also realized that if his friends decided to do something different from him, it was their prerogative.

Anthony put his friends down, blaming and judging them, because they didn't make the same choices or enjoy the same level of activity as him.

> ◀◀ Let's stop projecting our problems onto other people and start solving them ourselves.

Exercise

YOUR RESPONSIBILITY

1. Become aware of your thoughts and judgments about other people, and determine whether they are fact-based or subjective.

2. Change your subjective thinking into fact-based thinking.

3. Try to understand others, their reactions and their behaviour in certain situations.

4. Then, when you make a decision, be it for yourself or someone else, ask yourself what your responsibility is before judging others.

5. If things don't go the way you'd like, think before blaming the other person. Could you reconsider your decision?

6. How do old emotional wounds make you feel? Try to go beyond learned reactions and listen to what you truly want.

7. Why blame someone else or the situation? Try to understand what's really involved. What do you stand to gain by blaming someone else?

8. Find solutions, if need be, with the people involved. Opt for the best decision without blaming the other person.

REMEMBER: Why do we want to prove who we are? To prove that we exist. Why do we want to be irreproachable? To reassure ourselves, because we lack self-confidence, self-acceptance and self-love.

Playing the victim

*"Focus on what you have, not on
what you don't have."*

Is it in our interest to play the victim?

"Everything's going wrong. I got a flat tire. I lost my keys this morning. I always seem to get a control freak for a boss. Why does this only happen to me? I just don't get it. Some people seem to have all the luck!"

Are these really crisis situations? Or do we get something from playing the victim?

Playing the victim is a way of getting attention. But it doesn't solve anything. Is it in our interest to make other people feel sorry for us? For individuals who lack self-esteem, seeking pity is a way of establishing self-worth (they are the victims of other people's wrongdoing: other people are wrong, consequently they are right). Since others are to blame, the victim doesn't ever have to take responsibility for his or her situation.

It's difficult for us to assert ourselves when we're unable to recognize who we are. How can we then determine ways of fulfilling our desires and making ourselves happy?

Let's take time to listen to the messages we give ourselves and observe how we behave. We may seek pity, find reasons to be unhappy, blame our misfortunes on others. Conversely, we might pity others ("Poor you!"). What a message to convey to others—that they're powerless to make changes in their lives.

If we are to make changes in our lives, we must have a very deep desire to do so. If we are to make changes, we must modify attitudes that generate anger and frustration and that ultimately create an obstacle to our personal progress.

Verbalizing what isn't working in our lives is a good first step. What we do with it after that is a whole other matter.

How are we going to make a commitment to stop feeling victimized, to stop feeling sorry for ourselves about what we don't have? Let's stop thinking that other people's lives are better, and start facing our difficulties. This would open the door to greater self-awareness.

🧑 *Real-life case*

Jerry, an entrepreneur

Jerry has always been self-employed. When he sees a business opportunity, he's quick to seize it and try to turn a profit. He follows his instincts. Some of his projects have succeeded, others have failed.

He initially came to see me to review his time management for new projects. He didn't think he was being efficient.

During one of our meetings, Jerry said enthusiastically, "I have three new clients coming on board this month. With them, I'll be able to meet my financial commitments and invest more in business development."

However, the projects never got off the ground: either the clients didn't have the capital, or start-up was delayed. Jerry said, "I'm so unlucky. I do everything I can to make it work and everything gets delayed. I feel as if I'm always dealing with disasters. I was counting on these projects. I've run up against one obstacle after another. I work hard, no one can say I don't. And there's only me to pay the bills. This really puts me in a tight spot."

During our discussions, I learned that this was not the first time Jerry had encountered such problems. He felt sorry for himself essentially because of the outcome of the poor decisions he'd made.

Of course Jerry was ambitious and wanted to be prosperous. He was thinking big, but his team didn't have the expertise to achieve the goals he had in mind. He took on too many projects at a time and spread himself too thin.

Jerry would start a new project and would be sure that he could achieve the projected financial results within a certain time frame. He had to become aware of the vicious circle he'd created. His pattern had a negative impact not only on his financial well-being, but also on his attitude, decision-making, health and family.

Impactful questions

- What's your motivation for taking on several projects at a time?
- What do you get from feeling sorry for yourself when nothing seems to be working, for example, when you say that you're so unlucky?
- What decisions have you made in the past few years that have had a positive impact on your projects?
- What decisions have you made in the past few years that have had a negative impact on your projects? Why?
- On a scale of 1 to 10, what's your level of stress because of your business?
- In light of the facts, what are you going to do to avoid repeating these behaviours?
- What would your level of stress and energy be if you took on one project at a time?
- Who would contribute to the success of your projects?
- What strategy will you follow to stay on track?
- What steps will you take in the coming weeks to correct the situation?
- What positive results will you achieve through these decisions?

🎯 *Realizations*

- Jerry's motivation for taking on several projects at a time was to live comfortably and to build up a good retirement fund. The projects that had been successful had not required a large investment of time or money.

- Feeling sorry for himself gave him a way, although unconscious, of getting attention from others. He realized that it had become a habit.

- His level of stress was very high. He had taken on far too much work; he wasn't sleeping well and had very little quality time with his family.

- Jerry had not followed his business plan. He needed to adopt realistic strategies and review his risk management.

- He decided to consult a strategic and financial planning consultant so he could chart a new direction for his projects. He also teamed up with partners that would enable him to keep his projects on target.

Today, Jerry has consolidated most of his assets. He adheres closely to his business plan and has improved his strategic and financial planning.

He now devotes his energy to one project at a time and works with an appropriately skilled team. His health has improved, as well as his relationship with his family.

Real-life case

Joanne, married for five years

Joanne decided to consult me because she wanted to work on improving her overall level of energy. She admitted that she found her husband, Edward, demanding as well as draining: he seemed to need a great deal of her time and energy.

Edward was someone who didn't react well to stress. Joanne told me that when he was going through stressful periods, he would be curt or impatient with her and would sometimes sulk. "He's dealing with a bunch of challenges at the office," she explained. "The company he works for is reorganizing. He's reached an impasse."

Joanne felt like a Good Samaritan. "Poor him," she said. "He's constantly running into difficulties. He's so unlucky. What he's going through at work isn't easy. He deserves to be treated better than that; he works very hard and he's really good at what he does. I'll take care of him and help him."

Supporting Edward made her feel good but, at the same time, it was an enormous undertaking. Was she really responsible for solving her spouse's problems?

Joanne wanted to save her husband. She believed that she could help him find solutions, but doing so required a lot of energy.

(≡) *Impactful questions*

- What's your motivation for taking your spouse in hand?
- How do you feel when you see Edward in distress?
- What do you find satisfying about assuming responsibility for his problems?
- What's behind your supporting him?
- What would you lose if you stopped taking care of his problems?
- What are the consequences of continuing the way you are?
- What could you do to be more self-respecting?
- What steps should you take to meet your own needs?

(⚙) *Realizations*

- Joanne felt indignant about her spouse's situation. "He's worked so hard to get where he is. He's been recognized by the business community." She felt obliged to help him because he's her spouse. She saw it as her duty.

- She thought that if she helped Edward, he'd be nicer to her. It upset her to see him distressed and she felt bad for him. His stress created tension in their relationship and thus stress for her. She didn't like his attitude. She felt that he treated her irreverently.

- It was her responsibility to tell Edward that she didn't appreciate the way he behaved toward her. The help she tried to give him didn't make him treat her better. It was clear in this case that she had to become more assertive with her husband if they were to respect each other.

- It was not her duty to see to Edward's problems. Her duty was to take care of herself.

Making a change isn't always easy. Joanne had to muster up a lot of courage to do so. In hindsight, it was for the best.

As for Edward, he was responsible for his own problems and for making changes in his personal and professional life.

We tend to be somewhat unaware of our own needs and put our energy into meeting the needs of those around us. We can't save others.

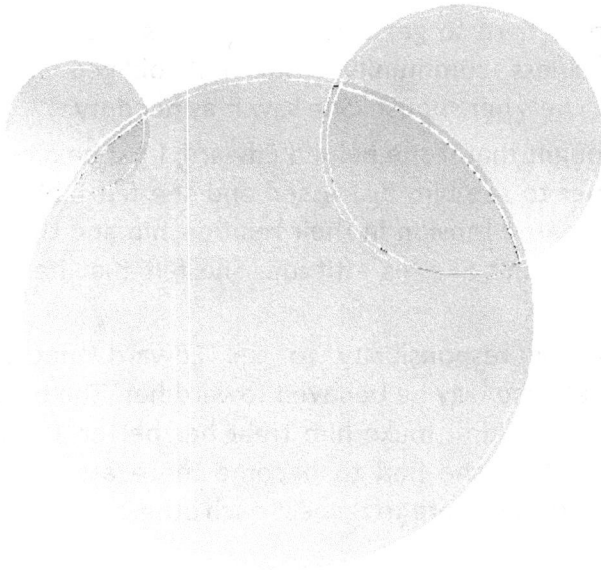

🧑 *Real-life case*

Susan, a photographer

Susan consulted me because she wanted to work toward her goal of meeting the right man. She had been involved in a number of relationships, but none of them had worked out. She said to me, "I just haven't been dealt the right hand. I keep meeting all the wrong guys. An exciting love life doesn't seem to be in the cards for me."

She'd intended to stay in her last relationship even though she was dissatisfied with it. It would have meant giving up on happiness.

I could see that Susan was playing the victim. She wasn't taking responsibility for her personal life.

📋 *Impactful questions*

- What's your definition of love?
- How would you describe your self-esteem?
- What do you value and expect in a relationship?
- How do you feel when you show your vulnerability in a relationship?
- How do you feel when you open your heart to someone?
- What do you fear and doubt in a relationship?
- What's your definition of commitment?
- What, in your view, are the steps that would lead to a commitment?

Realizations

- Susan was afraid of commitment. That was reflected in her fear of revealing herself and losing the person she allowed herself to love.

- It was threatening for her to show her vulnerability, and she reacted badly when her partners left her. She basically told herself, "If I allow myself to love someone, he'll leave me."

- Her father had left when she was very young, and she never saw him again. That had hurt her deeply.

- Susan attracted different men who had certain traits in common. Her relationships were always marked by the same dynamic—a lack of commitment.

- This repeated dynamic prompted her to take a look at her behaviour.

- Susan was able to identify where her behaviour was counter productive in a relationship and to make positive, appropriate changes.

Today, she no longer blames her relationship problems on fate.

We can progress from being a victim to gaining awareness. We are responsible for how we react in a given situation.

> Stop being a victim and
> start taking action.

Exercise

BEING IN TOUCH WITH YOURSELF

It's important to be in touch with yourself.

1. Take time to listen to the messages you give yourself and to observe how you behave.
2. Analyze the reason why you act like a victim or a saviour. Do you overestimate others or yourself?
3. Become aware of what you say and how you feel. Write those things down.
4. When you start feeling like a victim or feeling sorry for yourself, stop!
5. Why do you feel that way and why are you in that situation?
6. Look at how you behave in that situation.
7. Be aware of the options open to you to act differently.
8. Take concrete steps to break the vicious circle.

Rephrase statements you make so that they're more optimistic; that will prompt you to take action.

We have the power to change. Bemoaning our fate is futile.

REMEMBER: Let's say goodbye to sadness and take responsibility for creating the life we want. Let's develop the ability to appreciate and be grateful for what we have.

Find the love within you.

Being afraid

"Illusion is reality's border. Pierce fear to go beyond."

Deng Ming-Dao

Understanding fear

"I'm afraid of failing. I'm afraid of succeeding. I'm afraid of disappointing people. I'm afraid of dying. I'm afraid of change." Believe me, I listen to the messages I give myself too.

I've been afraid of tackling projects many times, including this book.

Sometimes we're afraid of making a change in our lives. What are we afraid of? The unknown? Our ability to complete a project, embark on an experience, take some action?

Fear is normal in certain circumstances, as it protects us. However, irrational fear is something else altogether. It can cause suffering, anxiety and physical as well as emotional pain.

If we never take the initiative and leave the security of our comfort zone, we'll never get beyond what ails us.

We don't need to be afraid. If we allow ourselves to be dominated by fear, it can be paralyzing and prevent us from doing something with our lives.

Fear is a stressful emotional state. We can encounter situations that pose a threat or danger to our physical or psychological well-being.

We respond to them by going into a specific emotional state and either confronting them or escaping from them. That's normal and even healthy, as it helps us overcome the threat or danger. However, when fear is irrational, it can paralyze us and prevent us from taking action:

Irrational fear = paralysis = lack of self-love

It's important to map out a way of facing the unknown. Do we need to determine the likelihood that what we fear will actually occur?

Fear is triggered by a potential threat. It generates the behavioural response of fight or flight. But flee what? Our own happiness? Our own achievements?

Why do we remain passive? Why don't we take action? Is the force of inertia so strong in us that we'd forgo our own happiness?

How many of our friends and family members decide to take the helm, change course and forge ahead?

What goes on in our minds? We think, "What's motivating them to take such action? They've got a lot of guts." In fact, they have faith in themselves. They've decided to take the leap and run the risks involved in the life choices open to them.

Your past   Your future

Your present

They've analyzed the situation; some of them have determined the worst that could happen in light of the decision they're making.

If we want to move forward, we have to leave our comfort zones. As mentioned above, irrational fear = paralysis = lack of self-love.

We can find any number of reasons not to take action. It's fascinating to see that when everything's going well, we don't take the time to think about our life. Shouldn't we be reflecting on it at all times?

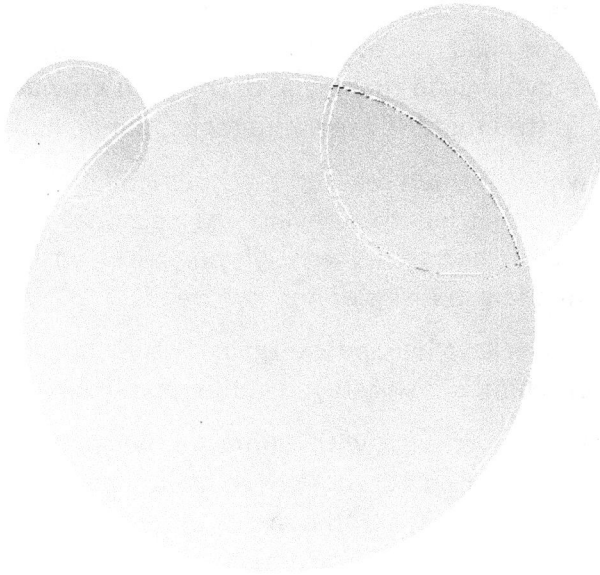

🧑 *Real-life case*

Carmen, a freelancer

Carmen wanted to have a fulfilling love life and was dissatisfied with the way she was developing as a person in her relationship. She wanted to leave her spouse, but couldn't bring herself to do so.

Carmen had been living with her partner for over ten years. She had stayed at home with their three children when they were young; that was the agreement she'd had with her spouse. When the children got a little older, Carmen found a part-time job. For the past couple of years, she'd felt that she and her partner had grown apart.

Carmen wanted something else, as some of her needs weren't being met. She had talked to her spouse about this: about changing the dynamic in their relationship and growing together. She had suggested that they see a therapist, but he had refused.

After a while, Carmen realized that they no longer wanted the same things. She tried to convince herself that she was the problem, that her hormones were playing tricks on her, that she was too demanding in terms of her own needs.

She tried to talk to her spouse again. She couldn't seem to get anywhere with him, but still stayed in the relationship.

She met a man at work with whom she became friends. They eventually got closer and Carmen developed feelings for him. She didn't want to be intimate with him out of respect for her partner and her own principles. However, that was the tipping point in her relationship with her spouse.

Carmen wanted to overcome her fear and leave her partner of ten years, with whom she had three young children.

Impactful questions

- What emotion do you feel when you think about staying in the relationship with your spouse?
- What can you still tolerate in the relationship?
- What prompts you to stay?
- What would you lose if you left your spouse?
- What would you gain if you left him?
- If you had a magic wand, what would you do to resolve your situation?
- What do you need to be able to leave?
- How would your spouse react if you left him?
- How would you like things to be once you've left?

Realizations

- Carmen was afraid; that prevented her from leaving.
- She admitted that she would miss the presence of others when she got home from work in the evening, the comfort to which she had become accustomed, and the big house on the lake.
- She would lose advantages, such as dinners out, treats and her comfortable financial situation, which would mean that she'd have to find full-time work. Family activities wouldn't be the same. She would also lose her dream of enduring love with one person.
- However, she would gain her freedom; she would have the liberty of choosing for herself.
- She dreaded how her partner would react. They'd met when they were teenagers, become friends, and then developed a relationship.

She didn't want to jeopardize the friendship part of their relationship. He would be upset and disappointed.

Can you relate to this situation? How many of us are prisoners of our own fear (fear = paralysis)?

How many people stay in relationships that are no longer working?

Six months later, Carmen decided to leave her spouse. She mapped out a plan of action. She found an apartment and asked her employer to give her more hours, which she was granted.

That required courage and perseverance, but also self-love. Carmen had to grieve her idea of a relationship, her ways of thinking, and her lifestyle.

Her leaving required many adjustments, including shared custody of the children.

Carmen has been on her own now for more than a year. She has met a suitable man, but they don't live together. She feels free and is blossoming in her new life, not stagnating in fear.

Taking responsibility starts with accepting who we are. Feeling responsible for our situation means taking our fate into our own hands. It all depends on us, and on our ability to change our attitude and ultimately the direction we're heading in.

🙎 *Real-life case*

Jenny, a manager

Jenny, a dynamic woman, came to see me to overcome her fears about her professional achievements. She was experiencing a lot of anxiety and her speech was pressured.

Although Jenny knew she had the skills she needed for a promotion, she was afraid to advance in her career. She had concerns about what her superiors and her colleagues might think or say if she succeeded.

Her fear of being judged by others was significant; leaving her comfort zone was even more frightening.

Jenny had started having trouble sleeping. During our appointments, she admitted that she fed off the approval and recognition of others: she didn't want to disappoint people and needed confirmation that she was doing a good job.

It was surprising to see how much Jenny depended on the praise of others. She had difficulty recognizing her own qualities and achievements.

☰ *Impactful questions*

- Why do you constantly need positive feedback from others to feel worthy?
- What do you get from it?
- How do you see yourself?
- What skills and abilities enabled you to obtain a management position?
- Why aren't you able to recognize your own worth as a person?
- How does that make you feel?
- What are your stress symptoms?
- What do you do to relax?

◉ *Realizations*

- Getting feedback from others made Jenny feel more secure about the decisions she made. It was very important to her to be liked by her employees.
- Jenny had difficulty finding the right words to describe herself. She said things like "Maybe I'm..." She realized that she didn't have a good sense of her own worth.
- Jenny became aware that she could give a long description of her accomplishments, but couldn't name her qualities.
- That made her very emotional. She was nervous and had difficulty concentrating. She realized that some of her feelings were unrealistic.

Nonetheless, Jenny was very determined to make changes and to get to know herself better.

She worked on certain aspects of herself using the mirror technique, which is a very powerful tool (see chapter seven).

We only see five percent of ourselves in the mirror; other people see the remaining ninety-five percent. We don't give this much thought, but it's significant.

Jenny and I also worked on her anxiety reactions. I asked her to draw up a list of her reactions to situations in different areas of her life (see chapter seven).

She became aware of how she felt in relation to her anxiety reactions. She ultimately included breathing techniques in her morning routine.

> « Anxiety can help limit danger. But if we overestimate the danger, anxiety will no longer protect us.

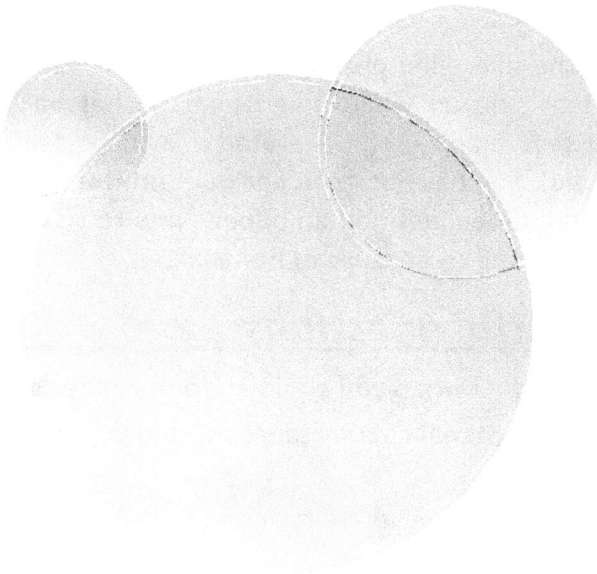

🔘 *Real-life case*

Julie, a lab technician

Julie came to see me because she wanted to overcome her fear of water.

Julie and her spouse had gone to the Dominican Republic a few years earlier and had stayed at an all-inclusive resort for a week. They had enjoyed water-based activities during their vacation. On the last day, they decided to go sailing on a 4.9 metre boat. It was a beautiful sunny day, but the wind was strong. The organizer had warned them to be careful, because the water was very rough.

Julie's spouse was a good sailor; however, they crossed the wake of another vessel and their sailboat capsized. They both ended up in the water. Julie struggled and panicked, but fortunately she had a life preserver. Her spouse was able to turn the boat right side up while Julie swam on her back to shore, despite her severe anxiety (accelerated heartbeat, feeling like she wanted to die). She has not gone back out on the water since the incident. Every time she's had an opportunity to go out in a boat, she's avoided doing so because of her anxiety.

🔘 *Impactful questions*

* How do you feel when you go down to the water's edge?
* Under what optimal circumstances would you go back out on the water?
* What's the challenge you're facing?

- What techniques could you use to eliminate fearful thoughts preventing you from going out on the water?
- What will you do to resolve this situation?

Realizations

- Julie knew that she needed to analyze her fear because it was irrational. Every time she had an opportunity to go out on the water, even under entirely safe circumstances, she refused.

- She felt fearful and anxious, and worried about losing control. This prevented her from looking at the situation objectively.

- Julie did some research on visualization and relaxation techniques to help her dispel thoughts that automatically entered her mind.

- She decided to create a strategy enabling her to become aware of her irrational fear and understand it. How was she going to stop the thoughts that went round and round in her head? Scenarios = emotions = fear = paralysis.

- During our appointments, we worked on a plan of action. Julie began using breathing techniques, evaluating situations involving a real threat and assessing the degree of danger. She became aware of her emotions. She even had someone accompany her who gradually helped her regain her self-confidence.

- Julie continually told herself that the present situation was in no way threatening and that it was vital to get rid of threatening thoughts that jeopardized her well-being.

That required a great deal of perseverance on her part. Julie is now able to go sailing again.

Exercise 1

YOUR ACTION PLAN

In order to face fears that create anxiety:

1. Write down a situation that causes you anxiety.

2. Note what goes through your mind repeatedly and become aware of those thoughts when the situation recurs.

3. Determine what triggers your anxiety.

4. Draw up an action plan for facing your fears. The action must be realistic and appropriate given your feelings. You want to make sure you can succeed.

5. What new thoughts have you become aware of?

Exercise 2

FEAR ASSESSMENT

1. Draw up a list of your fears. Observe and recognize the scenarios that repeat themselves.

2. Pay attention to your physical symptoms when you're experiencing fear.

3. When you make a decision, what negative scenario might enter your mind?

4. If you overcome your fear, what do you stand to gain or lose in that situation?

5. Be honest and see if you're prepared to experience the most negative scenario (positive = action). If not, determine how far you're willing to go.

6. Who or what controls your life? You or your fear?

REMEMBER: Fear is directly related to our perception of ourself and our faith in ourself.

Making excuses

*"Nothing seems true that
cannot also seem false."*

Michel de Montaigne

A few observations

Last year, at a business reception, I listened to some of my colleagues talk about what they'd do if they won the lottery. "Why, I'd..." "I'd buy my mother a house," "I'd have my freedom." What freedom was my colleague talking about? That was strictly a perception.

Not winning the lottery is no excuse for not pursuing your dreams.

I agree that we need money to live, but do we need to win big to start achieving our dreams? Lottery corporations advertise that we can make our dreams come true if we win the jackpot.

Let's say someone wants a large cottage. If the person is unable to buy one, he or she could rent one on a lake. That could be an option.

What prevents us from realizing our dreams?

Whatever the obstacles, the justification seems to come in the form of excuses. "I don't have time." "It's too demanding." "It's not the right time." "I have to put too much into it." "I can't do anything until the summer."

Is winning the lottery a solution to these problems? Fear = paralysis and excuses = paralysis.

We all have our reasons for procrastinating. We give other activities greater priority and thus avoid pursuing our dreams. We give excuses to justify why we're not doing what we say we really want to do.

This has an impact on every aspect of our being in every sphere of our lives. Do you make excuses for not pursuing your dreams?

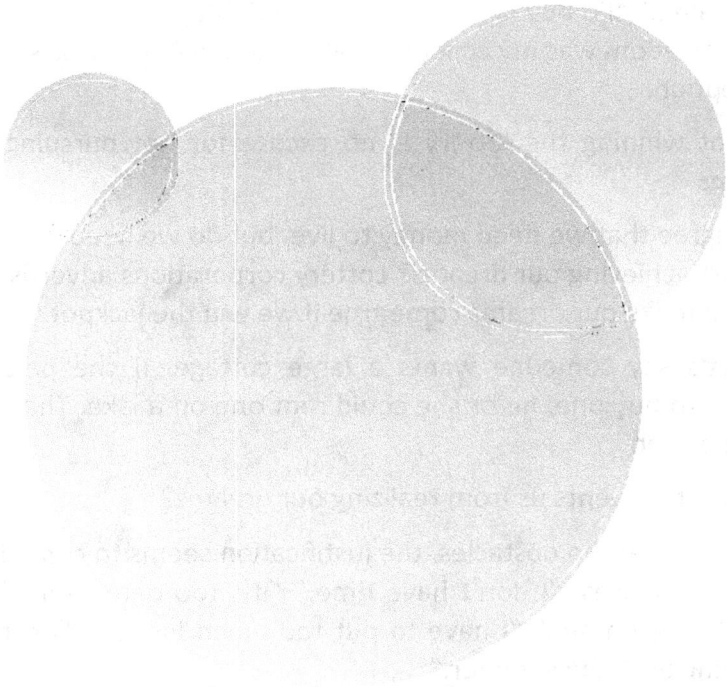

🧑 *Real-life case*

Sharon, a customer service rep and mother of two young children

Sharon came to see me because she wanted to lose weight. She had started a diet and an exercise program over two years earlier. She hadn't managed to follow her workout plan because she wasn't always very disciplined. She wanted to lose seven kilos and had met with a dietitian numerous times.

"It's because of my schedule. I finish work late. Last week, I got a call from my cousin and lost track of time. Then I was too tired to work out. I hadn't had dinner: I had to eat something because I was starving. My children needed me at home."

She gave me many excuses for not following her diet and exercise program.

≡ *Impactful questions*

• Why do you want to lose weight?

• Why are you not following your action plan?

• What are the challenges that prevent you from following your plan?

• How do you feel when you don't follow your plan?

• What do you gain from not following it and what do you lose?

• How are you going to make sure that you stick to your plan?

Realizations

- Sharon was determined to invest in her health. Her father had died of a heart attack at a young age. He had been overweight and inactive.

- She had been raised solely by her father. She didn't like to leave her own children strictly with their dad while she was out exercising. "I'm afraid they'll miss me. They're young. At the end of my work day, I don't have much time to spend with them."

- Sharon felt anxious because of this. She used avoidance strategies. Even though her husband was able to look after the children, she still felt that they needed her.

- I asked her when would be an ideal time to exercise; she then thought of a way she could work it into her schedule.

- She realized that she could get up a little earlier every morning and exercise for a half hour to her video. She told me that she had more energy at that time of day.

- Sharon added a breathing technique and some stretching exercises to stimulate her circulation.

- She also realized that with her busy schedule, she had to review her meals and plan them so that she would stick to three meals and three snacks a day.

All of this required discipline and perseverance; it proved how determined Sharon was to achieve her goal.

🛈 *Real-life case*

James, a baker

James got in touch with me because he wanted to review and update his plan for starting his own business. He'd been working as a baker for over ten years. He was very talented, a real artist. Customers gave him special orders for finely decorated cakes. He was valued by the owner of the bakery where he worked.

Coming from a family of entrepreneurs, James had been wanting to start his own bakery for the past few years. It had been his childhood dream. Although his father gave him sound advice, he wasn't sure he was ready to take the leap.

During one of our meetings, James said to me, "I'd like to be my own boss, but maybe I'm still too young; maybe I just don't have the nerve. I think I'll keep working and save for the next couple of years. I'm not sure I have enough experience, so maybe I should wait." He found all sorts of excuses for putting off the project, even though he was very enthusiastic about it. I knew he had his doubts—that was clear from what he said and his tone of voice.

☰ *Impactful questions*

- Why do you want to set up your own bakery?
- How do you feel about having your own business?
- What are your key skills and abilities for managing such a business?
- What are the skills needed by an entrepreneur?
- Why do you keep putting off opening your own bakery?

- What are the obstacles you're facing?
- What changes could you make to reduce your stress?
- Who are the people you need to start setting up your business?
- How will you ensure that your business will succeed?
- What are you risking if it doesn't work out?

Realizations

- James really wanted to start his own business and fulfill his potential. However, he was afraid of the unknown and felt stressed by it: he didn't know if he'd be a good boss and manager. Still, he acknowledged that his father had suggested competent people to oversee the operational and financial aspects of the business.

- James recognized his skills and was recognized by his peers, since he took care of the bakery when his boss was away on vacation. He came up with new ideas for increasing sales, had good business sense, and made sure that the bakery was profitable.

- He looked into business start-up grants, applied for some and received grant money. He assessed the risks and was ready to take the step.

- The main obstacle for him from the beginning was not wanting to disappoint his father, whom he idolized. James was very proud, and it was important for him to succeed. He needed his father's approval.

- Today, the business is doing well and James has the right people helping him. Gone are the excuses.

🢂 *Real-life case*

David, a land surveyor

David wanted to take his personal life in a new direction and came to me for support.

David was very fond of his wife; they'd been together for more than twenty years. However, their relationship had become one of friendship only. He stayed in the marriage because he felt that his wife had always been there for him. He wanted to help her with her problems, as she had helped him. "I just can't see myself leaving her after all we've been through. She wouldn't be able to take it."

"I've talked to her about separating. She got very emotional and said, "You want to leave me? To walk out on me? I need you." He felt guilty, so he put off ending the marriage. That went on for more than five years.

David wanted to change his situation, but was reluctant to take the plunge.

🗏 *Impactful questions*

- What's your definition of happiness?
- How do you feel in this situation?
- What makes you stay with your wife?
- What do you want most at this point?
- How do you want to live your life?
- What's your responsibility in all of this?
- What resistance are you facing?
- What are the consequences of staying with your wife?

- What positive aspects would come from ending the marriage?
- What prevents you from taking the big step?
- What measures will you take in the next few weeks?

Realizations

- What David wanted most was to live on his own and to find himself. He realized that he wasn't responsible for how his wife felt.

- He also realized that if he stayed in the marriage, he'd die inside.

- David was afraid to leave his wife because of how people would judge him. He didn't know if his friends and family would accept it or how his children would handle it. He felt guilty about how others would react.

- He realized that he was afraid of the unknown. Even though he wanted to leave, he continued to procrastinate. He became aware of all the excuses he'd been making. He wasn't in control of the situation.

- David decided that he was going to sit down with his wife and discuss the decisions he'd made.

- He then moved into a small apartment until the house was sold. That enabled him to see his situation more clearly, to figure out what he wanted in life, and to be able to move forward.

- David let go of all the excuses, which wasn't easy, and took the leap.

Exercise

DEMYSTIFYING YOUR EXCUSES

1. Take a sheet of paper and write down a specific goal.
2. Ask yourself the following questions: What need is this goal satisfying? What do I want to change or achieve?
3. List the excuses that prevent you from achieving the goal. For example, fear of what your family will say, being humiliated by them, not having enough money, not making the right decision or not being up to the task.
4. How do you feel about these excuses?
5. Take the time to think about them and to analyze them in detail. What are you resisting?
6. What's the worst thing that could happen if it doesn't work out?
7. What would be the positive aspects of taking action? Dreaming is one thing, but dearly wanting something is quite another.
8. What are you going to decide for yourself?

Take a look at what's preventing you from pursuing your goal. This will enable you to see if you're at peace with the changes you want to make.

As I've mentioned, excuses are paralyzing. Once you demystify your excuses, you'll clear the way for taking action and pursuing your dream.

This exercise can be confusing initially, but will ultimately enable you to see your situation more clearly. After several months of rolling up your sleeves, you'll be able to see the progress you've made.

Having expectations

"With expectations, you suffer so much from the absence of what you desire that you cannot tolerate the presence of another."

Marcel Proust

Self-assertion

Are we really being genuine when we agree to do things? Do we make some decisions based on the wishes and desires of others?

Do we assert ourselves and our needs? Asserting ourselves means being able to stand up for ourselves and make choices.

"I did it because she asked me to." "I thought it would please her." "Did it really please her?" Do we want to be liked or loved *at all costs*? I think this goes back to childhood. We all needed to be loved by our parents, so we behaved in ways that met with their approval.

At some point, don't we all have expectations of others? People act toward us according to how we act toward them. Are we able to set boundaries?

🔘 *Real-life case*

Jeanne, a mother

Jeanne came to see me because she wanted to work on her goal of having more harmonious relationships with her family and friends.

She felt the need to settle her conflicts with others, and could see that she was the one making waves. During one of our meetings, she told me how upset she was that her husband had not sent her flowers for Valentine's Day. A few days before February 14, Jeanne had started imagining scenarios and had expectations because her husband, Charles, gave her flowers every year.

This year, Charles made a dinner reservation for them at a restaurant. Jeanne was disappointed. She had an idea in her mind as to what she wanted the day to be like. Dinner out did not entirely coincide with her plan.

«

> ## Unmet expectations = disappointment = frustration

Jeanne had expectations of her husband as well as other people. When her expectations weren't met, she created conflict and had no qualms about saying things like "I would have liked you to..." "You could have..."

I could picture how Valentine's Day went with her husband. Instead of recognizing what she had—an intimate evening with Charles—she constantly focused on the fact that she hadn't received flowers.

Jeanne had to learn how to accept other people as they are, so she could have smoother relationships with them.

≡ *Impactful questions*

- What's behind your expectations?
- What do you need to let go of, if you want to have more harmonious relationships?
- What steps could you, yourself, take to ensure your expectations are met?
- What are your expectations of your husband?
- What happens if things don't turn out the way you planned? What then?
- What makes you think that your husband should live up to your expectations?
- Why is it so important that things happen the way you want?

Realizations

- Jeanne didn't think that her husband loved her the way she loved him. She knew, however, that he loved her in his own way. When she was young, she suffered deeply from a lack of recognition.
- Jeanne felt that her husband didn't give her enough recognition. She wanted more.
- She could buy herself flowers. She could organize her recreational activities herself, so that she wasn't always depending on others.
- Jeanne realized that her husband had the right to express himself in his own way. She needed to be grateful for what she had, and not focus on what she didn't have. She acknowledged that there are many ways of doing things, not just her way.
- Finally, she acknowledged that a little gratitude goes a long way.

Real-life case

Drew, a technician

When Drew first consulted me, he told me that he wanted to improve the way he planned and organized his time.

As we worked together, it became clear to me that the issue wasn't his planning and organization. The problem was that he never said no to anyone, and thus created the expectation that he'd always be available.

Drew was nice, helpful and easy-going. Everyone—his family, friends and colleagues—said he was a good guy.

Even his wife's friends were constantly saying, "Wow, I wish I had a man like that. He's so nice!"

Drew couldn't say no to people because he didn't want to disappoint them. He met everyone's expectations but his own. As a result, he felt stressed and frustrated because he wasn't doing what he needed to. That, of course, had an impact on his time management.

Not long ago, Drew's lifelong friend, Joe, asked Drew to help him with his home renovation project the following weekend. Drew said, "I'll have to think about it and get back to you." Joe egged him on, saying, "Oh come on, Drew, you know we work well together. It'll be fun! Bill and Rob can't come that weekend. You can't let me down!" In the end, he said yes.

Drew had to give a presentation at the office the following Monday morning. He had to work really hard Sunday night and get up at 4:30 Monday morning to finish the presentation. It was very stressful for him.

He was tired, and angry with himself because the presentation wasn't quite up to scratch. Although the meeting went well, there could have been repercussions.

Drew needed to become aware of the expectations he was creating. That took him some time. I asked him to do some exercises and to make sure he followed up on them.

Although Drew was altruistic, he needed the time and freedom to do things for himself.

Impactful questions

- Why do you agree to do everything your friends and family ask?
- How does that make you feel?
- What do you need to change so that you can meet your own obligations and deadlines?
- How would your friends and family react if you asserted yourself and gave priority to what you want or need to do?
- Would they be less grateful if you sometimes said no?
- Why do you have such a deep need for other people's approval?
- What do you need to be able to say no to others?
- How could you go about asserting yourself?

⚙ *Realizations*

- It wasn't easy for Drew to simply say no, because he'd created expectations for so long. He had to be very assertive.

- It was interesting to see Drew stand his ground when his friends and colleagues made different demands of him.

- He understood that he had a deep need for other people's approval. He didn't want people to judge him or to think poorly of him. He wanted to be liked and loved.

- Drew realized that he'd made people somewhat dependent on him. He had to overcome his need for approval.

- After planning and organizing his schedule, he decided to adhere to it, and to meet that commitment to himself.

- His wife, family and friends adjusted to Drew's new behaviour. He's still a nice guy, but he's now fulfilling his responsibility toward himself and has regained control of his life.

If we stay in a dynamic where we're meeting other people's expectations and not our own, we'll never achieve the happiness we seek. By taking responsibility, we can be grateful to others and, at the same time, feel better about ourselves.

🗣 *Real-life case*

William, an artistic director

William needed the tools to deal with a situation involving his father, and came to me for help. The youngest of six children, William was spending a lot of time with his father, as he had with his mother before she passed away ten years earlier. All of his siblings live outside the city.

Every time his father asked him to do something, William was there to lend him a hand. But with his wife expecting their second child and needing more help, he felt he couldn't be there for his dad as much. He didn't know how he could refuse his dad anything, and he felt stuck.

🗐 *Impactful questions*

* Why do you feel stuck?
* How do you react when your father asks you to do things for him?
* What emotions do you experience when he asks for your help?
* What are your father's expectations of you and your siblings?
* What difficulties do you anticipate now that you won't be as available to help your father?
* How are you going to tell your father that you won't be as available for him?

Realizations

- William didn't want to disappoint or displease his father; he had always been there for him. However, he had to respect and assert himself. He thought his father would be upset and stop speaking to him. His siblings could pitch in. The family could prepare a schedule together and everyone could help take care of their father.

- Solutions were now open to him.

- William met with his siblings to talk about their father's changing needs. He explained the situation to them and they had a good discussion. Then he spoke to his father. To his surprise, his father understood the situation, even though he was a little sad because he was used to having William around.

- William asserted himself and learned that his father still loved and accepted him.

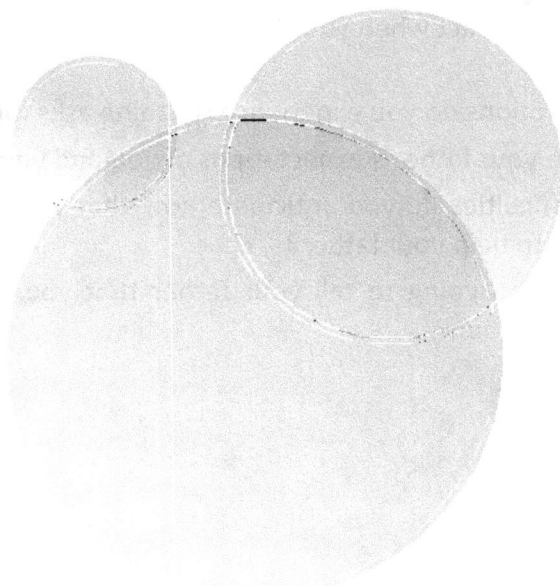

Exercise 1

YOUR EXPECTATIONS OF OTHERS

1. Why do you have expectations of others?
2. Are you passive or assertive?
3. Write down your answers to the first two questions and explain why it's important for you to be aware of them. Did you lack recognition when you were younger?
4. Remember, everyone is unique and has their own way of seeing things.
5. If your expectations in a given situation are not met, what is there in that situation that you can still appreciate?

Exercise 2

OTHERS' EXPECTATIONS OF YOU

1. Listen to the requests that other people make of you.
2. Take time to think about them; don't give your answer too quickly.
3. Determine whether you really want to do something for the person; if you don't, then refuse.
4. Be aware of how you feel. Why do you think you feel that way?
5. Try to grasp why you feel the way you do.

These exercises will enable you to understand what's behind expectations, and to realize how important it is to remain true to yourself and feel that the decisions you make are the right ones for you.

Not living in the present

"You can always cope with the Now, but you can never cope with the future... The answer, the strength, the right action or the resource will be there when you need it, not before, not after."

Eckhart Tolle

Today's world

One day, I drove to work and, for some reason, had no memory of the drive from my house to the office.

I was thinking about what had happened with the children the day before and what would happen at the office meeting that day.

I was remembering how I'd felt and how I would feel, without knowing what was going to happen.

Have you ever experienced a situation like that?

Choosing to be in the here and now isn't easy: it means learning to live in the present, to be in the moment without being in the past or the future; it means being aware of your body at all times.

I know that's difficult and requires an ongoing effort. It's not easy to focus on your physical sensations.

Look at the new generation. They're on the phone when eating out with their friends, checking their text messages. They're always doing more than two things at once: watching television, playing on their iPad, iPod or iPhone. They're constantly solicited by their devices.

Are we incapable of concentrating on one thing at a time? The way we choose to use new technology doesn't help us live in the here and now. Even before these devices existed, we were continuously thinking about the past or the future. Are we unable to live in the now? It's a challenge for everyone.

A few months ago, I read an article about a teenage girl who died in the subway because she was looking down at her iPod and stepped between two cars instead of onto one.

How many times do we text or read our messages while driving? I admit that I'm no exception. How many people have had accidents because of it?

If we don't live in the here and now, how can we take responsibility for creating the life we want to live? We experience a type of duality. We think about the past, about our childhood wounds. We live with old sorrows that prevent us from moving forward. We fantasize about the future to escape the present. It's a deadly pattern.

Exercise

THE HERE AND NOW

1. What are you paying attention to right now?
2. Is your mind wandering even as you read this?
3. Take a deep breath and feel the effect within your body.
4. What's going on within you? Do you feel comfortable being present? Are you thinking about the past or the future?
5. Try to keep your focus within yourself and not outside yourself.

There are many books on the market that deal with the present moment and introduce readers to meditation. I meditate every day and I see a difference. I regain a sense of calm, which enables me to stay focused on what I'm doing. I'm not saying that it's always easy: it requires concentration and discipline.

Self-Esteem

As I briefly mentioned at the beginning of chapter one, self-esteem is central to the individual and at the heart of self-sabotage.

Many books have been written by psychiatrists and psychoanalysts on the topic of self-esteem. They suggest that self-esteem stems from the interaction between self-confidence, self-respect and self-assurance, and that it enables the individual to progress and succeed. Self-esteem is made up of self-love (knowing your worth), self-perception (how we regard ourselves and our behaviour) and self-acceptance (recognizing our likes, interests, strengths and weaknesses). We have seen all these aspects at play in the real-life cases provided in chapter one.

Self-esteem appears early in childhood and plays an important role in the development of the individual; it is constantly changing. It is built on the basis of our own beliefs, what others say about us, what others say directly to us, and what others have done to us (for example, rejecting us in certain situations).

Low self-esteem is expressed through doubt, indecision, vanity and even contempt. People suffering from low self-esteem may feel sad, angry, rejected, jealous or inferior to others.

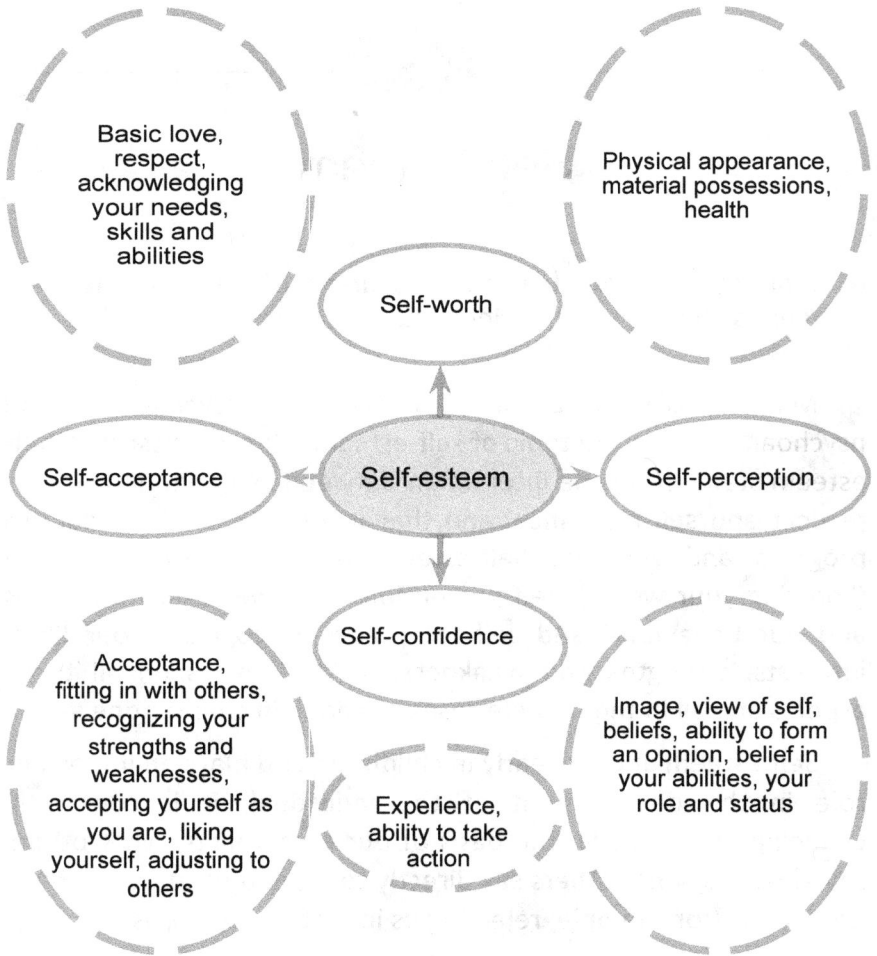

It's important to show young children affection, to help them become aware of who they are and the qualities they possess, to help them develop their creativity, to suggest goals that they are capable of achieving. Sometimes we overprotect our children when we should be letting them learn from their mistakes. That would strengthen their self-confidence and image.

If a youngster has a balanced childhood, can he or she become a balanced adult? I believe so. Do we sometimes have doubts? Yes, and that's normal. However, it's essential not to sink into a quagmire of doubt if we want to progress.

People with positive self-esteem are able to assert themselves, deal with events as they arise, make decisions, take action and respect others.

People with positive self-esteem fit in with others socially. They adjust and are able to recognize others. They aren't afraid of their friends and family, and don't need to promote themselves to impress others.

Remember, we are the result of how we perceive ourselves. And that affects the way others perceive us.

Self-esteem must be maintained. It doesn't remain constant throughout our lives.

Self-esteem can have many guises. Just because someone has a university degree doesn't mean that he or she has positive self-esteem. Negative self-esteem can hide behind various achievements.

A person's self-esteem can be compared to a computer hard drive. We all have computer files dating back several years which we can retrieve any time. We also have antiviral programs to protect our data.

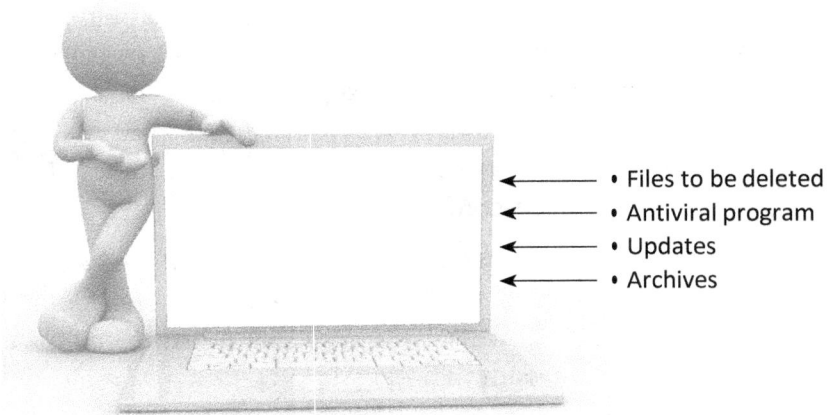

- Files to be deleted
- Antiviral program
- Updates
- Archives

We can delete some files that we're not using and make room for new ones.

The same applies to people; we record all the experiences in our lives, from birth to present.

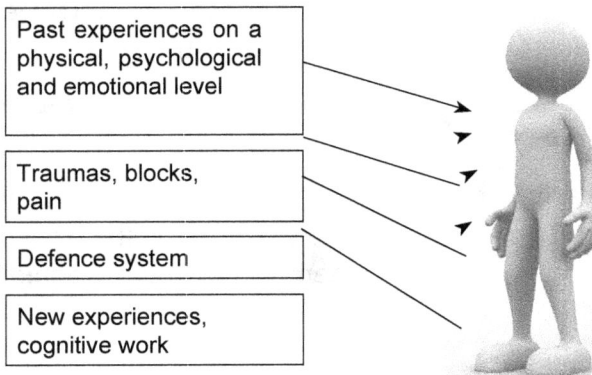

Past experiences on a physical, psychological and emotional level

Traumas, blocks, pain

Defence system

New experiences, cognitive work

Having experienced pain, we put up barriers and build defence systems. But we also assimilate new experiences.

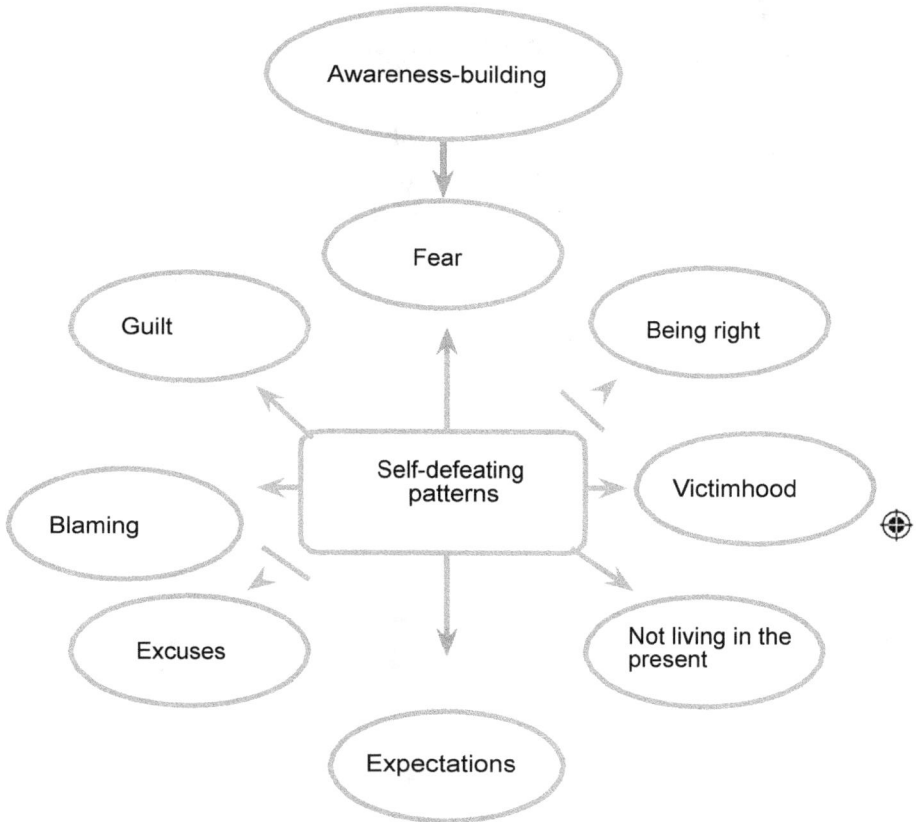

Some of the people in the cases discussed in this book did not have positive self-esteem. They had often received negative messages about how they were perceived. However, they became aware of this and were able to move forward and find practical ways of improving their well-being.

It's important for us to get to know ourselves and to recognize the values we hold dear.

Our thoughts are often responsible for our lack of confidence. It's therefore vital to develop our awareness and change negative thinking into realistic, positive thinking.

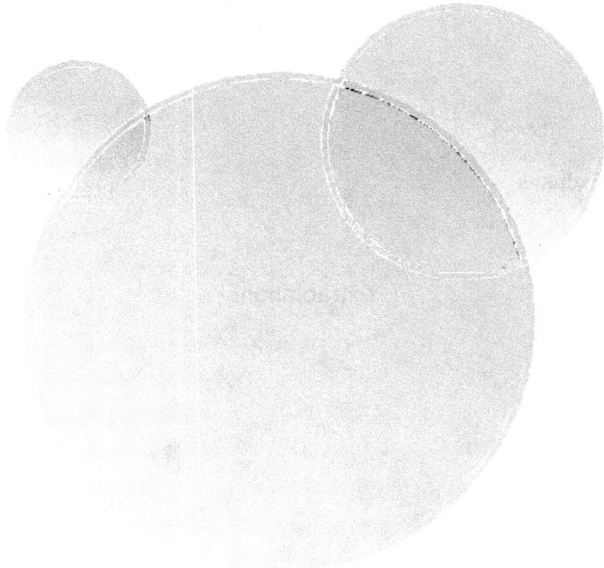

Exercise

POSITIVE THINKING

- Take the time to think about your environment, be it at home, school or work. Is it positive or negative? Do you feel good in it?
- If some situations cause you negative feelings, write them down.
- Determine whether your thinking is realistic. If not, replace it with more accurate, positive thinking.
- Pay close attention to your senses, to what you see, hear, smell, taste and touch.
- Surround yourself with people who support you and encourage you when things get rough. Spend as little time as possible with people who are negative and critical.

As you have seen, the people discussed earlier in this book took action, which enabled them to have more realistic and positive thoughts about themselves.

Developing a positive attitude will enable you to gain confidence in yourself and will give you the impetus to achieve your goals and be successful.

Don't give up. It's worth the effort!

3

Resistance

As we have seen, people can initially show resistance to making certain life changes. That resistance can surface when the time comes to take action toward our personal or professional goals.

People will find a thousand and one reasons for putting up resistance and not pursuing their goals. Then they simply run away from them and abandon them altogether. Some of the people discussed earlier had to overcome considerable difficulty to achieve their goals, but they decided to persevere and push ahead.

Why are people so resistant to the changes they want to make in their lives? Is it because of the measures they have to take? The challenges they have to overcome?

Take, for example, all the effort the people discussed earlier had to make to be able to move forward. They exercised discipline, followed up on what they talked about with me during our appointments, and became more aware of their needs, motivations and desires. All of their efforts paid off.

Some people didn't want to know where their beliefs came from, while others wanted to analyze their challenges. In all cases, they reacted to their situations.

At the end of the day, it enabled them to grow and to broaden their way of thinking.

Freedom or Imprisonment?

You think it's only in prison that people find themselves behind bars? Think again!

A couple of years ago, I had to decide whether to accept changes to my job conditions after my employer restructured. I would have had to work longer hours and travel more, which would have affected the quality of my personal and professional life.

I could have coped with the changes for a few years for financial reasons. But at what cost? I didn't want to feel like I was on a diving board, just bouncing up and down. I finally took the plunge, and rejected the new conditions. I didn't have another job to go to, or a safety net in place.

Of course I was frightened at the beginning. But I felt compelled to listen to my intuition and follow my instincts.

I had confidence in my skills, abilities and experience. I'd wanted to start a consulting practice, and now the time had come. I've never regretted my decision, because I like what I do. Above all, I feel free.

Had I accepted the new job conditions, it would have been against my will. I would have remained in a prison of my own making, with all the fear, blame, excuses and lack of self-confidence that it entails. How many people would like to leave the prisons they've created for themselves?

- Being right is more important than...
- Fear is more important than...
- Excuses are more important than...
- Blaming yourself or others is more important than...
- Playing the victim is more important than...
- Feeling guilty is more important than...
- Having expectations is more important than...

LIVING THE LIFE YOU WANT?

Follow your instincts.

I remember watching a show on marine biology. The people on it talked about the jobs they loved. One of them said, "I intuitively do what I like, without asking myself too many questions. To me, it's as natural as breathing!"

Freedom is being able to follow your instincts.

Tickets to the Show

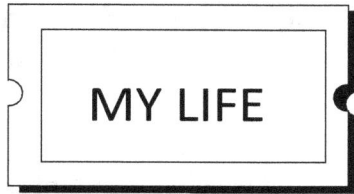

MY LIFE

When we buy tickets to a show, be it to a concert, dance or play, we have expectations: we read the reviews in advance and the program before the show starts.

Let's say that our lives are a show and that we have a ticket to see it. Our show, like any other, is divided into acts. What role do we want to play in this show? How do we want to play it?

Which acts do we think should be included on the program? What would make us applaud at the end of the show or even give a standing ovation?

We come into the world, we're raised by our parents, who instill values in us as well as perceptions. We do as they ask; some people become what their parents would have liked to be.

How do we see ourselves? How do we want to live our lives?

We can accomplish so much. Are we realizing our full potential?

Do we believe in ourselves strongly enough to make a change? What do we expect from life? What relationships do we want to have?

To make a change, we need to develop our awareness and adopt a positive attitude.

Did you know that, according to one Stanford Research Institute study, 87.5% of people's success can be traced to their positive attitudes, while only 12.5% is based on their skills and knowledge?

I'll ask the question again: Who are we? What, within us, is genuine and will not change? What is our intuition telling us?

If we want to make a change, we need to adjust our thinking, to modify what we visualize. To want what we want.

Let's go to where we want to be.

« And leave our egos behind.

We all possess something that enables us to be greater. We all have the power to grow in our environments.

Gaining awareness enables us to get to know ourselves better. Once again, that requires practice, perseverance, discipline and, above all, self-love.

« We are love. We have consciousness. Let's use it.

Being Responsible

Are we able to take risks? How do we deal with a situation that we don't like?

It's important to consider it a challenge, a difficulty we can overcome. That's what enabled the people discussed earlier to leave their comfort zones and see their real strengths in achieving their goals.

We all fail to take responsibility at times. It can be tempting to blame others, to feel guilty or to play the victim. We experience this very often both at home and at work.

We are the architects of our own lives. It's essential for us to focus on our strengths and on what we can do to take up our challenges.

The issue is not so much what happens to us, but what we can do with what happens.

We need to know what we want to accomplish. Becoming aware of our positive energy will enable us to achieve what we want.

I cannot stress enough that

> We need to surround ourselves
> with positive people.

I make sure that my clients work on their goals by using positive statements rather than negative ones.

We all have dreams and we can all realize them. However, we need to focus on what we truly want. How do we do that? By developing an action plan that is specific, measurable, attainable, realistic and timely. It's what I call the "SMART plan."

I often ask my clients, "If you had a crystal ball and could see six months into the future, what goal would you like to have achieved?"

Whether we'd like a promotion, a new house or a slimmer figure, being able to see that goal reached is effective. It helps us visualize an ideal situation and find potential ways of achieving it. When we see an ideal future, we're able to eliminate censorship and obstacles.

In fact, the client is the one who discovers the new approaches.

First, we have to ask ourselves the questions: What's the most important thing to me? Then, would I be happier? What do I truly need?

Let's say I buy a new pair of figure skates. Will that make me a better skater? Even if the skates enable me to be a better skater, I have to ask myself if that's the most important thing to me.

> « What is my basic motivation for achieving happiness?

How do we measure success? My father used to say to me, "Give it your best," "Believe in yourself," "Try to achieve what you really want." That attitude was less stressful for me than wanting to succeed at all costs. At the end of the day, the most important thing is to be true to ourselves and make choices that reflect who we really are.

How many times have I seen parents force their children to achieve what they would've liked, rather than letting their children achieve what they want?

I'm from that generation of parents. Performance and success are still of prime importance in our society today.

When I was young, I wanted to become a musician, to have a career in music. My mother said, "You can't earn a living that way! Take a secretarial program and you'll be able to work anywhere."

I see parents force their children to play hockey, football or violin because they wanted to do that but didn't have the opportunity. They impose their dreams on their children.

Let's take time to listen to our children. What would they like to achieve? It's so important to encourage them in what they want to do. For me, that's part of success.

Tools

Optimize your energy
so you can live the life you want.

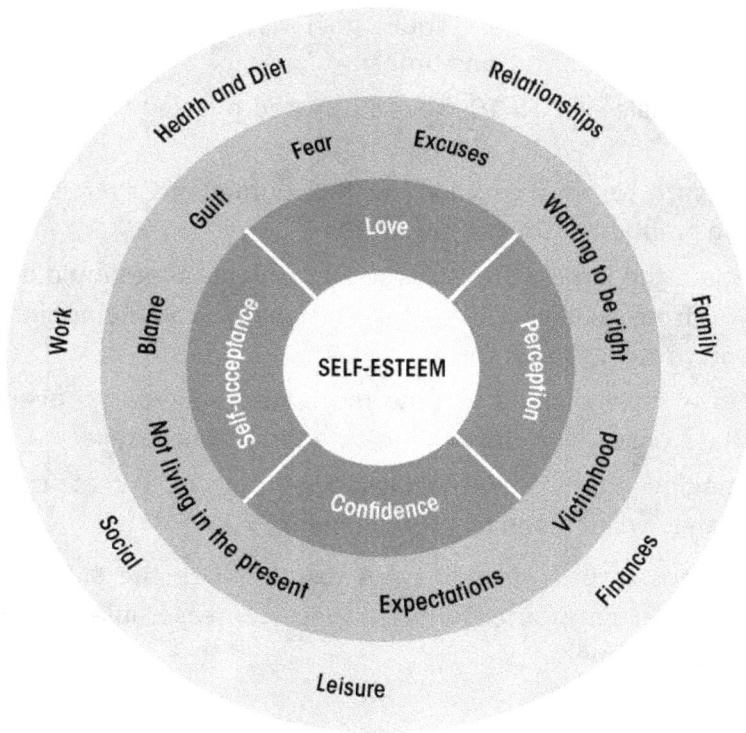

Components of self-esteem (self-acceptance, love, confidence, perception)

Types of self-sabotage

Spheres of life

Self-esteem

Exercise 1

THE SMART PLAN

How do you make sure you have more energy?

1. Choose the sphere of your life that is a priority for you to work on.

2. Choose a goal in that sphere. Using the SMART plan, determine whether your goal is specific, measurable, attainable, realistic and timely.

3. On a scale of 1 to 10, how motivated are you to achieve this goal?

4. Be sure to observe how you feel during this exercise. Name the emotions using simple words.

5. Name the largest obstacles within yourself that would prevent you from achieving this goal. This will help you pinpoint what you're struggling with.

6. On a scale of 1 to 5, how motivated are you to overcome these obstacles? This will indicate the action to take.

7. Imagine that you've achieved your goal. What concrete change will it make to your lifestyle?

What measures do you need to take? Use the SMART plan, because these measures must be specific, measurable, attainable, realistic and timely.

(✎) *Exercise 2*

THE MIRROR

Some people use the mirror technique to develop a more positive relationship with themselves. This technique has produced some very beneficial results.

The exercise is as follows: stand in front of a mirror for ten minutes and simply stare at your pupils. While doing so, open your heart to the person you really are without judging.

It will take you a few sessions to feel comfortable with the exercise. It took one of my clients four sessions before she could actually do it.

It can be a challenge: some people can't even look at their reflection when they start the exercise. They're unable to look at themselves outwardly or inwardly.

It's fascinating to see how many managers have difficulty seeing themselves as they are.

Once you feel comfortable with the exercise, start talking to the different aspects of yourself (for example, the good you, the bad you, the strong you, the weak you).

Work on asserting your qualities, appreciating yourself and accepting yourself.

Practise the exercise using "I" (for example, "I believe in myself," "I can") and you'll notice a difference within a few months.

As you become more grounded and self-assured, you'll be able to progress and blossom in your personal and professional life.

If you practise this exercise, you'll awaken your self-awareness, see yourself differently, leave your comfort zone and become more empowered.

It's not easy to leave your comfort zone, but the uneasiness you feel is temporary and will pass. Then you'll be able to pursue what you set your sights on.

Exercise 3

AWARENESS OF ANXIETY REACTIONS

The exercise consists in identifying and noting what's bothering you and preventing you from achieving your goals on the following levels:

- Conscious: What's unsettling about how you feel? Are you feeling defensive? Are you having unrealistic feelings?
- Cognitive: Are you having problems concentrating or remembering things?
- Perceptional: Are you imagining worst-case scenarios or losing control?
- Emotional: Are you nervous, tense, anxious, worried or impatient? Are you having difficulty sleeping? Are you having nightmares?
- Behavioural: Are you speaking quickly or hyperventilating?
- Physiological, cardiovascular: Is your heart beating quickly? Are you having dizzy spells?

• Respiratory and dermatological: Are you having coughing fits or breathing quickly? Are you having skin reactions (sweaty palms, flushing, excessive perspiration, itching, etc.)?

Exercise 4

WORDS AND SPEECH

Sometimes we're unaware of how we express ourselves, the words we use, and the power of those words.

1. Take the time to become aware of how you express yourself.

2. Identify any negative statements you make about yourself, such as "I'm incapable," "I'm too old," "I can't." Eliminate them from your vocabulary.

3. Replace them with positive statements like "I want," "I'd like," "I can."

Take five minutes every morning to say these positive statements.

Be affirmative. If you become aware of the positive things you say, rather than the negative, you can reprogram your mind for positive thinking.

Start with statements like "I like myself," "I'm a good person," "I'm strong," "I'm capable," "I'm going to attain..." "I trust myself," "I'm healthy," "I accept my life and I'm going to change what I don't like."

We don't realize the power of the words in the messages we give ourselves. They have an incredible impact on how we act and behave. They also have an impact on others.

We underestimate the power of the words we use: we create entire worlds with them.

> ## We are bound by the limitations that we create. Our words can help give us the power to overcome them.

Exercise 5

FIVE STEPS EVERY MORNING

Breathe

Take time to breathe deeply for five minutes when you get up in the morning and go to bed at night. Breathing is important. I do this exercise with my clients before each coaching session.

The goal: five minutes of calm = being present = having a clear understanding = impact.

Think positive thoughts

Say positive thoughts out loud like, "I'd like to stay healthy," "I will stay healthy," "I'd like to find love," "I will find love."

Move your body

Get up and move. Make sure you exercise at least five minutes a day, by walking, stretching or whatever you like.

In the morning, I put on some music I enjoy and do exercises to it.

Be grateful

I say "thank you" out loud for everything I have and everything I do. I encourage you to do the same every day. Be grateful for everything that enables you to lighten the load of more difficult situations.

I belong to myself and everything I need is within me. For that, I am grateful.

Visualize

Visualize your goals. Create a clearly defined image in your mind of the things you want to have and to do. Hold onto that image and thank the Universe, because those things are achievable.

I suggest to my clients that they illustrate what they want, through drawings or collages. That allows them to see it every day and thus increases their chances of achieving it.

Under each illustration, write a title and a phrase summarizing what you desire, or a personal, inspirational message.

Hang the illustration in your bedroom or office where you can see it. Once you've done this, you'll have taken a big step toward mentally building your future. That will propel you forward. I believe in the law of attraction, according to which you can attract everything you desire provided you believe in it, think about it, and persevere.

Cut photos out of magazines or newspapers, tape them to your illustration, and add positive comments. Some people do this every year with specific goals, because it helps them attain them.

Conclusion

The mind is key. When we fill our minds with courageous, optimistic thoughts, we become highly effective.

Remember, we're the ones who create the model for our lives. We have a treasure trove within us. Even if we experience failure, we can start over again.

In this book, I've suggested some exercises that can help you have a better life. Start doing these exercises so you can move forward. Start taking action and continue taking action.

Find new freedom within yourself. That's what I wish for you.

Be uniquely yourself and be happy!

In *Eat, Pray, Love*, Elizabeth Gilbert writes: "If you are brave enough to leave behind everything familiar and comforting and set out on a truth-seeking journey (either externally or internally), and if you are truly willing to regard everything that happens to you on that journey as a clue, and if you accept everyone you meet along the way as a teacher, [then]... you are prepared—most of all—to face (and forgive) some very difficult realities about yourself."

> The truth will never be withheld from you.

Recommended Reading

Auger, Lucien. *Vaincre ses peurs*. Éditions de l'Homme.

Brennan, Barbara. *Guérir par la lumière*. Éditions Sand.

Bungay Stanier, Michael. *Do More Great Work*. Workman Publishing Company.

Coit, Lee. *Listening: How to Increase Awareness of Your Inner Guide.* Hay House.

Cyrulnick, Boris. *Les Nourritures affectives*. Éditions Odile Jacob.

Hay, Louise. *You Can Heal Your Life*. Hay House Inc.

Hill, Napoleon. *Think and Grow Rich*. The Ralston Society.

Jacobs, Gill. *Chronic Fatigue Syndrome: A Comprehensive Guide to Effective Treatment*. Element Books Ltd.

Johnson, Spencer. *Who Moved My Cheese?* G. P. Putnam's Sons.

Lowen, Alexander. *Bioenergetics*. Arkana.

Mallet, Xavier. *Paroles pour décideurs*. Lavoisier.

Morency, Pierre. *Ask and You Shall Receive*. Transcontinental.

Pittman, Frank. *Grow Up! How Taking Responsibility Can Make You a Happy Adult*. St. Martin's Press.

Ponder, Catherine. *The Dynamic Laws of Prosperity*. DeVorss & Company.

Quoist, Michel. *The Meaning of Success*. Fides Publishers, Inc.

Shapiro, Debbie. *Your Body Speaks Your Mind*. Sounds True.

Tolle, Eckhart. *The Power of Now*. Namaste Publishing.

Ulrich, Dave, Smallwood, Norm and Sweetman, Kate. *The Leadership Code*. Harvard Business Press.

www.ingramcontent.com/pod-product-compliance
Lightning Source LLC
Chambersburg PA
CBHW070250290326
41930CB00041B/2432